Thriving, *in the* Black

ROBERT S. DAYSE

Copyright © 2024 Dr. Robert S. Dayse. All rights reserved. No part of this publication may be reproduced, distributed, or transmitted in any form or by any means, including photocopying, recording, or other electronic or mechanical methods, without the prior written permission of the publisher, except in the case of brief quotations embodied in critical reviews and certain other noncommercial uses permitted by copyright law. For permission requests, write to the publisher, addressed "Attention: Permissions Coordinator," at the address below.

ISBN: 979-8-9902680-8-1

Publishing By: DemiCo National, LLC

www.DemiCoNational.com

TABLE OF CONTENTS

Introduction, *Page 8*

Chapters

1. Wealth Within Your Reach, *Page 16*
2. The Power of Financial Affirmations, *Page 35*
3. Employment & Entrepreneurship, *Page 73*
4. Starting the business of YOU, *Page 113*
5. Choices & The Ability To Harness Your Inner Superpowers, *Page 154*
6. Marriage & Partnership, *Page 176*
7. The Magical Rule of 72 Made Easy, *Page 188*
8. Achieving Financial Freedom & Investing, *Page 203*
9. Providing Value and Growing Your Income, *Page 222*
10. Financial Success & Your Future, *Page 248*

About The Author, *Page 272*

SPECIAL THANKS & DEDICATIONS

To my beautiful wife, Jaclynn Dayse, whose unwavering support and nurturing spirit have helped shape the next generation.

To our sons, Robert, Michael, Matthew, and Myles Dayse, you are the best and a blessing that brings joy to our lives.

To my mother, Sharon Dayse, who has been my guiding light and guardian angel in the flesh. Your love and wisdom continue to inspire me every day.

To my sister, Dr. Sharon Avenot, and my brother, Kelvin Dayse, for their constant encouragement and support throughout this journey.

To Loleta Ferrell, I could not have done this without you! Thank you for listening, never giving up on me, and always believing in my potential.

I am grateful to family members and authors Janelle Williams Henry, Brittany Jackson Crudupt, and Dr. Anthony Dayse, whose work has been a source of inspiration and guidance. Your contributions have paved the way for my journey.

Special thanks to Ms. Patricia Sprye, whose endless creative energy and insightful feedback have been invaluable.

To Benjamin Avenot, thank you. Your efforts have made this book better than I could have ever imagined.

To the countless others who have lent their support, directly and indirectly, thank you for being part of this journey and helping me thrive in the black.

-Robert

INTRODUCTION

Where you start in life does not determine your endpoint. Our destiny is shaped by our actions, not by our origins. This book explores a naturally occurring pattern; a way of thinking, acting, and communicating that empowers people to inspire those around them. While some are born with different talents and may have an inherent ability to inspire, this skill is not exclusive to them. We can all learn this pattern. With a little discipline, any leader can inspire others, both close to them and around them, to advance their ideas and vision. We can all learn to lead and add value to the lives of others.

The goal of "Thriving, In the Black" is not merely to get rich but to enrich your life and the lives of the people you care about. Let's start by fixing what's not working in addition to reinforcing what is already working. This book serves as a guide to focus on and enhance the positive aspects of our lives and businesses. Its aim is to learn how to ask better questions and act. Often, we begin attempting to answer the wrong questions or misunderstand the root problems.

The theme of this book goes beyond mere survival; it empowers people to thrive and flourish. By offering a roadmap to financial freedom, this book outlines practical steps for people to achieve wealth and financial independence. It emphasizes the importance of smart financial management, strategic planning, and disciplined execution. In essence, being "in the black" in various aspects of life implies achieving positive outcomes, whether it's financial stability, health, relationships, personal growth, career success, time management, or emotional well-being. It signifies a state of balance, growth, and overall flourishing in different domains of life.

"Sometimes when you're in a dark place you think you've been buried, but you've been planted."

-Christine Caine

"Thriving, In the Black" explores the metaphor of being in a dark, confined space not as a hindrance but as a vital stage of growth and opportunity. This perspective shift is crucial for anyone navigating the turbulent waters of financial challenges or personal setbacks. It posits that these challenging times are not about being buried under problems but about being planted in the fertile soil of potential.

Just as a seed thrives in the darkness of the soil, businesses and individuals can also see their darker periods as crucial for germination and growth. In the financial realm, the goal is to be "In the Black," a state symbolizing profitability and stability. This book illustrates how apparent darkness can be a foundation from which to rise. The roots of a tree, though out of sight, are vital for its growth, anchoring the tree and absorbing nutrients. Similarly, our challenges can root us in essential values and strategies, reinforcing our determination and capacity to flourish despite adversity.

The book encourages embracing these periods of darkness as opportunities for planting the seeds of future success. By viewing our trials as foundational, we can transform them into the bedrock of a thriving, profitable state, both personally and professionally. "Thriving, In the Black" teaches us to appreciate the unseen growth happening beneath the surface, much like the sturdy roots of a tree that allow it to reach towards the sky. Thus, in moments of doubt or difficulty, remember you are not being buried; you are being planted, poised to grow into a prosperous future loaded with possibilities.

"Thriving, In the Black" is a crucial foundation for passing on generational wealth. It goes beyond just handing down money and property. It's about sharing values, wisdom, abilities, and support from one generation to another. While money matters, generational wealth is about more than that. It's about passing on intangible assets like love, spirituality, practical know-how, and strong relationships. These non-material things are just as important for building a lasting legacy and ensuring the well-being of future generations.

The most tangible form of generational wealth transfer involves the passing down of assets, investments, properties, and financial resources from parents to their children. Financial wealth provides opportunities for future generations to access education, start businesses, invest in their futures, and achieve financial security.

Parents are our first leaders, often passing down their values, beliefs, and principles to their children, shaping their worldview and guiding their behavior. This can include ethics, integrity, responsibility, compassion, and cultural or spiritual beliefs. Instilling these values in the next generation helps maintain family identity and fosters a sense of continuity across generations. Parents pass down practical knowledge, skills, and expertise acquired over their lifetimes to their children. This can include professional skills, trade skills, problem-solving abilities, and practical life skills such as cooking, gardening, and home maintenance. Passing on such knowledge equips future generations with the tools they need to succeed in their personal and professional lives. Parents provide emotional support, love, and nurturing to their children, laying the foundation for their mental and emotional well-being. Positive relationships between parents and children contribute to a sense of security, self-esteem, and resilience that can benefit individuals throughout their lives. Families often pass down social connections, networks, and relationships that can provide opportunities and support to future generations. These connections may include friendships, professional contacts, mentorship, and community ties. Leveraging these relationships can open doors to educational, career, and personal opportunities. Parents pass down cultural traditions, rituals, and spiritual beliefs, which are integral to the family identity and heritage. These traditions help preserve cultural heritage, strengthen family bonds, and provide a sense of belonging and continuity across generations.

Generational wealth transfer is a multifaceted process that involves the transmission of both tangible and intangible assets from one generation to the next. By passing down financial resources, values, knowledge, and relationships, parents can empower their children to build upon the foundation laid by previous generations and create their own legacy of success and fulfillment.

For example, just like in the Cherokee tradition of fathers guiding their sons through a transformative journey into the forest, passing down not only practical skills but also wisdom and character traits essential for their growth into responsible men. Fathers would lead their sons into the woods. After finding a secluded spot, the father would sit his son on a stump and blindfold him. Fathers would then whisper in their sons' ears a promise to return at dawn. The father would then leave the boy to face the silent wilderness alone.

Throughout the night, the boy would sit in quiet contemplation, his senses sharpened by the darkness. Every rustle of leaves, every whisper of wind became amplified in the stillness. In that loneliness of night, he would grapple with his fears and uncertainties, listening intently to the symphony of the night. As the first light of dawn pierced through the blindfold, the boy would remove the blindfold to find his father sitting beside him, a silent guardian throughout the long night. In that moment, he understood the essence of manhood, the courage to face adversity, the strength to endure, and the wisdom to seek guidance when needed.

Inspired by this ancient rite of passage, both parents, especially fathers, today embark on a similar journey with their sons, guiding them through a carefully crafted program that encompasses the essential elements of manhood. Fathers play a pivotal role, leading their sons on a joint exploration of modern manhood, while also supported by mothers in this endeavor. Together, they embrace and instill values such as integrity, responsibility, respect, and empathy, ensuring a well-rounded upbringing that prepares their sons for the challenges and responsibilities of adulthood. Through hands-on experiences, parents equip their sons with practical life skills like cooking, cleaning, home repairs, financial management, and car maintenance, ensuring they're ready for the demands of adulthood. Fathers prioritize their sons' physical and mental well-being, engaging in fitness activities, discussing nutrition, and promoting healthy habits. They foster open communication, guiding their sons to navigate emotions, resolve conflicts, and build strong, respectful relationships. Imparting crucial financial wisdom, fathers teach budgeting, saving, investing, and the importance of hard work and financial independence. By leading with honesty, integrity, and moral courage, fathers set an example and engage their sons in discussions about ethics and values. Supporting their sons' personal growth, fathers encourage goal setting, resilience, and exploration of interests, nurturing well-rounded individuals.

Together, fathers and sons volunteer in the community, instilling a sense of responsibility and compassion. Acting as positive role models, fathers provide guidance and encourage their sons to seek mentorship. They create opportunities for reflection and celebration, boosting their sons' confidence and sense of achievement. Maintaining open communication, fathers offer ongoing support and mentorship tailored to their sons' individual needs, fostering understanding and acceptance. Through this transformative journey, fathers and sons cultivate a profound bond rooted in love, respect, and shared experiences, preparing the next generation of men to face life's challenges with strength, integrity, and compassion.

One recurring theme that consistently emerges from these conversations is the fear of the unknown. Fear affects different facets of life, from entering new relationships to making financial decisions and even considering educational pursuits. Often, fear becomes a significant roadblock hindering people from realizing their full potential.

Dr. Dayse discovered that many people are apprehensive about their financial futures. They are unsure how to manage their money, invest wisely, or plan for retirement. This uncertainty significantly hinders their financial well-being, prompting him to act. Driven by the need to bridge the wealth knowledge gap, Dr. Dayse embarked on a mission to share knowledge and provide guidance. He believes that by doing so, he can empower people to make informed decisions about their wealth and finances. His goal is to keep them "In the Black" and demystify the beliefs of success, money, and wealth formation.

Through a journey of continuous learning and self-improvement, Dr. Dayse expanded his own financial knowledge and understanding. He attended seminars, read books, and sought advice from financial experts. He realized that to help others, he needed to equip himself with the right tools and information. As he gained more expertise in personal finance, he started incorporating financial discussions into his daily conversations. He began sharing insights, answering questions, and providing guidance to clients who were eager to learn.

Over time, Dr. Dayse began offering financial workshops and seminars for his clients and the community. These sessions cover topics like budgeting, saving, investing, and retirement planning. He brought in financial experts to share their knowledge and insights. He finds it heartening to witness the positive impact these workshops have had on people's lives. Through his efforts, he has seen individuals transform their financial situations. They have become more financially literate, started investing wisely, and taken steps to secure their futures. The fear of the unknown has gradually receded, replaced by a sense of empowerment and control. Dr. Dayse's experience as a healthcare professional has taught him that sometimes, all it takes to make a significant difference in someone's life is a willingness to address their fears and provide them with the tools they need. Closing the financial unknown gap is an ongoing mission for him, and he is dedicated to helping as many people as possible find financial confidence and security.

In the chapters that follow in "Thriving, In the Black," Dr. Dayse shares some of the key lessons and insights he has gathered on this journey. These lessons go beyond money; they are about overcoming fear, embracing knowledge, and taking control of your financial destiny. He hopes readers will find them valuable as they embark on their path to wealth and financial freedom.

How to Get the Most Out Of "Thriving, In the Black"

Be curious and eager to learn: Approach the book with excitement and a desire to understand and utilize the ideas it shares. Knowing these principles can make a big difference in your life.

Keep coming back to the book: Read it again and again, not just once. Regularly revisiting the book will help you remember and understand the important ideas.

Put the ideas into action: Try to apply what you learn in your daily life. Consider how you can implement the suggestions in real situations.

Check how you're doing: Every week, think about how well you've used the ideas and what you can improve. Learn from any mistakes you make.

Write it down and make a list: Take notes on the important parts of the book. Create a list of the ideas you want to use in your life.

See it, Do it, then Teach it: To maximize the benefits, immerse yourself in the concepts, apply them actively to your life, and then share your newfound wisdom with others to solidify your understanding and create a ripple of positive change. Teaching others can help you understand the ideas better.

By following these simple steps, you can utilize the wisdom from "Thriving, In the Black" to improve your life and become a better person in various areas, such as your relationships, work, and family.

CHAPTER ONE

Wealth Within Your Reach

Have you heard the tale of the farmer and the baker? Once, there was a farmer who sold a pound of butter to a baker. One day, the baker decided to weigh the butter to see if he was getting the right amount. The baker confirmed that he was receiving less than a pound of butter from the farmer. He was angry about this, so he took the farmer to court. The judge asked the farmer if he was using any measure to weigh the butter. The farmer replied, "Your Honor, I am primitive. I don't have a proper measure, but I do have a scale." The judge asked, "Then how do you weigh the butter?" The farmer replied, "Your Honor, long before the baker started buying butter from me, I have been buying a pound of a loaf of bread from him. Every day, when the baker brings the bread, I put it on the scale and give him the same weight in butter. If anyone is to be blamed, it is the baker." Remember this, my friends, in life and in business; you get what you give. Don't try to cheat others.

The story of the farmer and the baker teaches us an important lesson about reciprocity and integrity, which are fundamental principles for "Thriving, In the Black." Just as the farmer gave the baker the same weight in butter as the bread he received, in life, we often get what we give. When we act with honesty, fairness, and generosity, we create a positive cycle of reciprocity that benefits both ourselves and others. Conversely, attempting to cheat or deceive others ultimately leads to negative consequences, as seen in the case of the baker's attempt to cheat the farmer.

Therefore, by embodying values of integrity, honesty, and fairness in our interactions with others, we not only uphold our own ethical standards but also contribute to the well-being and prosperity of our communities.

> *"We make a living by what we get, but we make a life by what we give."*
>
> -Winston Churchill

We live in a world where choices and opportunities are abundant. A world where one bad choice, coupled with one missed opportunity, can feel like the end of the world. Setting the stage minute by minute and hour by hour for confusion about money. Like, where did it all go? These feelings are common. So, you are forgiven for believing that life is a series of trial and error with no real and true answers about moving forward in life with fewer blunders. But this is a false truth I want you to dispel from your weary mind. So, for a moment, let's take a step back from our past doings so we can move forward with more financial clarity. Let's lay out a plan for making money in a way that feels right and is understandable to you. May this book be a beacon of clarity for all who seek it.

The timing of our life's journey isn't always as straightforward as we imagined. Sometimes we hit detours, get flat tires, and take unexpected turns. These events can leave us feeling frustrated and increase self-doubt. However, in these moments, it's important to remember that God's timing for our life is better timing. Your life is a masterpiece and not a cheap trinket. One step forward with sound knowledge is better than taking 10 steps without a clear purpose. Additionally, it's essential to remember that when things don't go as planned, it doesn't mean that something went wrong. It's an opportunity to have faith and extract valuable lessons from the experience. Too often, we mistake a season of growth for a season of setbacks, and we give up too early, especially when we have so much to gain. Use this time to seek wisdom and gather information before taking your next step.

There's a ton of great material out there on success, leadership, and creating wealth. Yet sometimes it feels like these resources are pulling you in opposite directions, which can get pretty confusing. One book might push you towards the executive path to success while another whispers about investing, mergers, acquisitions, or even quitting your job to start your own business. Some tell you to follow your heart; others emphasize crafting a business plan or discovering your life's purpose. You'll find authors passionately urging you to take bold risks while others advocate playing it safe with small, measured steps. The noise can leave you feeling lost.

Life can sometimes be puzzling, like a complex maze. There are so many choices, decisions, and things pulling us in different directions. But let's be honest: what we truly need amidst all this chaos is clarity. We need a personalized map that guides us. Today, we're leaving the confusion behind, breaking away from the norm, and finding clarity in our unique path.

Currently, you live in a landscape where choices and opportunities seem to overlap in an unpredictable mess—a mess only decodable by the world's most brilliant minds. But the truth is that these choices and opportunities are nothing more than a language you don't yet speak fluently. You speak at an elementary level, however you are in high school. Time to get you caught up. The good news is you have a good foundation. You've been dealing with the difficulties of money throughout your life. You've sought advice on managing finances, earning money, and spending. If you've been wise, you may still have some of that money saved. If this describes you, you're in a more advantageous position than you might realize. This book is designed to both give you information and organize your current thoughts and knowledge about money and life. The goal is to assist you in recognizing where to place your money based on your current circumstances and your future goals and needs. Let's get you on the path to financial success.

In this world, there are plenty of ready-made blueprints and celebrity-backed plans. These plans are not for you. Too often, these cookie-cutter molds have a certain amount of assumed knowledge, rendering the book or advice useless to most readers. Additionally, many money "experts" craft blueprints that take no consideration of your very distinct challenges, dreams, and goals. So it's up to you to do it for yourself. We are together daring to break free. Why? Because your journey is uniquely yours. Your aspirations, your strengths, your passions—they all combine to create a fingerprint that is yours alone. You are your best executive.

It's time to trade confusion for purpose and the generic for the genuine. Your dream and vision deserve an extraordinary path. This is where you shift from following someone else's script to writing your own epic tale. But let's not kid ourselves; crafting your own path is no walk in the park. It takes courage, introspection, and an unwavering belief in yourself. It requires stripping away the noise and focusing on what truly matters. And that's where clarity steps in. It's that magical moment when the fog lifts and suddenly you see your way forward with crystal clarity.

So, let's roll up our sleeves and design our personalized map. Let's pinpoint the milestones that matter most to us. Let's envision the destination and chart a course that's uniquely ours. It's about living authentically, making choices that align with our values, and staying true to our North Star. As you embark on this journey of crafting your path, remember that clarity is your most valuable asset. It's what will keep you on track, guide your decisions, and remind you of your purpose when the road gets tough.

The journey to financial freedom often begins with overcoming tough challenges, not just a big idea or new job. It's about committing to your dreams, calculating your Financially Unrestricted Number (FUN Score), and creating a solid plan to reach it. This process isn't about sacrifice but about letting go of things that don't serve you. Growing your funds should be rewarding. As you move closer to your goals, the journey becomes enjoyable, setting the stage for even more ambitious achievements. That's when "YOU Enterprises" truly takes shape. No more settling for less and hoping that a job, business venture, or side gig will eventually lead you to financial freedom. Instead, let's harness our strengths and focus on what truly resonates with us. Let's create a vision and strategic plan that consistently boosts our personal net cash flow every 90 days.

Stay alert, check your progress every week, and keep a scorecard. You'll be amazed at how in just 30 days you can turn things around and achieve a positive cash flow. It's a powerful step towards taking charge of your financial journey and building a pathway to real wealth and freedom. So, let's set off on this exciting journey of growth and empowerment, one step at a time.

When developing your FUN Score and crafting a life that aligns with your aspirations, there's no one-size-fits-all formula. Inside each of us lies the potential to create something amazing. The key is to seek help. Ask for guidance and listen to your trusted advisors.

Think of their advice as a map and your guides as your GPS. Each piece of advice works when you're on the right path, but it might not fit if your direction changes. For example, even if you're driving well, it doesn't help if you're supposed to go West but you're heading East. To get the right directions, you need to know where you are and where you want to go. Picture this: you're winning the game of life, nailing personal growth, conquering the professional front, rocking that thriving marriage, and even acing the whole parenting deal. But here's the secret sauce: it's all about that laser-focused mindset and strategic moves. It's not just about being busy; it's about being productive, aiming high, and stepping out of your comfort zone to win!

Let's break out of your shell. Not a seashell from the beach, but a metaphor for change and its powerful impact on your journey. Imagine you're in a cozy shell, feeling snug and safe. The problem is, there's no room for growth or progress. The shell is your comfort zone, but it also risks making you stagnant. Embrace change, break free from that shell, and suddenly, the world is your oyster. Don't just embrace change, thrive on it!

Is knowledge enough? Knowledge is like a hidden treasure chest filled with all sorts of valuable gems, facts, skills, and incredible insights. It's like a secret sauce that makes us unique and sets us apart from all the other creatures on this amazing planet. Just think about it: while we might not have the physical strengths of some animals, we have this incredible power within us—the power of complex knowledge. Knowledge so great we have built machines to carry us to the moon without growing wings. Knowledge so vast we can swim with fish without gills. And all it took to achieve the miraculous is the will to do so. Education is like having a superpower that allows us to learn, grow, and achieve things beyond our wildest dreams. So, let's unlock that treasure chest and use the power of knowledge to make our mark in the world! Sure, we might not have eagle eyes or the muscle of a superhero, but we've got something even more powerful—the magic of knowledge.

Just think about it. Even though we're not the strongest beings out there, we've got this incredible ability to learn, educate ourselves, and take charge of our lives thanks to the power of knowledge. Ever heard the saying "knowledge is power"? Well, think of it as a sneak peek into a superpower that's already within us. Through education, we can become the rulers of our own lives. We learn, grow, and then pass on all that amazing stuff to the next generation. It's like holding the keys to nature's biggest secrets, using them to make our lives even better. And when we apply what we've learned wisely, we're setting ourselves on the path to happiness and success.

Now, we're talking about knowledge—the kind of stuff you find in books, from teachers, or even online. But here's the twist: just knowing things isn't the end game. It's like having a toolbox but never actually using the tools. Real power comes when we take what we've learned and put it into action. We're not just collecting facts; we're turning those facts into something absolutely awesome.

As a wise individual once said, "Knowledge without action is like a book unread." In our age of information abundance, we have the incredible power to acquire knowledge with just a few clicks. However, possessing knowledge is merely the tip of the iceberg; it's what we do with that knowledge that truly matters. Therefore, don't limit yourself to being an information consumer; instead, harness that knowledge to effect real change in your life and the world around you.

In the world of personal finance is where financial wisdom merges seamlessly with the art of reinforcement. In this realm, knowledge alone can only take you so far. Sure, you can delve into countless books, watch numerous videos, and attend seminars on money management, budgeting, investing, and financial planning. You can become a walking encyclopedia of financial facts and figures. But guess what? That's just the starting line of the journey.

The real challenge doesn't lie in the accumulation of financial knowledge; it lies in the reinforcement of that knowledge, embedding it in your mind, your routines, and your bank account. It's about converting all that theoretical wisdom into practical actions that genuinely impact your financial well-being.

We understand. Personal finance can be overwhelming. It's like attempting to assemble a colossal jigsaw puzzle with pieces scattered in every direction. There's budgeting over there, investment strategies lurking in the corner, debt management hiding under the couch, and retirement planning stashed away in the closet. It's enough to make anyone's head spin. But fear not, we're here to assist you in breaking down those financial barriers, one practical step at a time.

So, why should you care about reinforcing information? Because financial knowledge without action is like a car without gas—it might look fantastic, but it won't take you anywhere. If you've ever felt inundated by the sheer volume of financial advice out there, or if you've set financial resolutions only to see them fizzle out, know that you're not alone.

In this journey, we'll delve into the art of reinforcing information in the realm of personal finance. We'll dive into the science of how your brain processes financial information and, more crucially, how to make that information stick. We'll tackle the nitty-gritty of budgeting, saving, investing, and planning for your financial future, all with a conversational flair and a practical focus. So, whether you're just starting on your financial voyage, striving to climb out of a financial pit, or aiming to elevate your financial game, this book is your companion. It's a straightforward guide that strips away the complexity and distills the essentials of personal finance into a language you can grasp.

It's not just about what you know; it's about what you do with it. That's where the real magic happens. Knowledge alone is like an undiscovered treasure. To make it a reality and change the game, we must bridge the gap between knowing and doing. That's where understanding, wisdom, and respect come in.

In "Thriving, In the Black," we're not just gathering information; we're using it to transform life into something extraordinary. Remember, knowledge isn't just something cool to have; it's an untapped resource ready to be unleashed. Let's make it count and turn that knowledge into a force that shapes our lives in amazing ways! You know what else? Knowledge is the key to any long-term success. It opens doors to fresh opportunities for upgrades, improvements, and change. But remember, you've got to take that next step in the process of change. In "Thriving, In the Black," we call it the application of information—taking what you know and putting it into action to make a real difference. So dive in, own it, and let's turn those challenges into opportunities and your opportunities into reality!

Ever feel like you're stuck in the mud, trudging through debts and financial stress? Well, you're not alone. Many of us have been there, and it's not a fun place to be. But guess what? There's a way out a path to financial healing and prosperity that doesn't require a degree in finance or a magical money tree.

You can heal your wealth. In this journey, we're going to explore how you can mend your relationship with money, abundance, and financial wellbeing. We'll skip the corporate jargon and dive right into the practical steps and transformative wisdom that can help you turn things around. So, if you're tired of feeling weighed down by financial worries and are ready to take charge of your financial destiny, stick around. We've got some valuable insights and benefits to share.

Imagine your life as a vast network of pathways, each leading to your desired destinations. Just as you sculpt a map to navigate your way, think of building the business of YOU as crafting an interactive guide for your life's journey. As you move toward uncharted horizons, every step shapes your story. Envision a place where the sky is a canvas of vibrant colors. This destination takes form with each brushstroke of your imagination. Now, you might question how business principles relate to your personal life. Let's look closer at how they are connected.

Are you living life to the fullest, or do you find yourself stuck in a rut? Pause for a moment and think, "What is it that you truly desire?" Take a minute or two, put pen to paper, and try capturing the essence of your life's goal. Whether you're envisioning the present, the near future, or the years ahead, the question remains: What is it that you want? As you flip through these pages, you'll uncover an intricate web that brings these concepts together. Discover how simple principles can infuse into every cell, giving your life a boost.

> *"Embrace life's blemishes; they are merely brushstrokes on the canvas of life!"*
>
> -Dr. Robert S. Dayse

Elevate Your Place in the World

In our complex world, we move through a society that is divided into different levels of social status. Among these, the concepts of class and caste stand out, each playing a significant role in defining personal identity, social interactions, and economic opportunities. Let's take a look into the dynamic world of class systems, shining a light for anyone aiming to improve their social and economic position, no matter their race, color, belief, sexual orientation, or where they come from. Here, we focus on empowering you to transcend your born status and achieve the life you envision for yourself through the malleable avenues of class mobility.

At the heart of class systems lies the principle of fluidity. Unlike the rigid birth-assigned strata of caste systems, class is influenced by a combination of economic, social, and educational factors. This fluid structure offers a beacon of hope the possibility of ascending the social ladder through personal effort, education, and financial success. The boundaries that define each class are permeable, allowing for movement not just between adjacent rungs but potentially over multiple levels driven by ambition and achievement.

The journey of elevating one's class is not merely about amassing wealth; it's about embracing the opportunities for education, professional development, and societal contribution. This path champions the ideals of meritocracy and equal opportunity, acknowledging that while systemic inequalities may exist, the avenues to overcome them are also within reach. It's a call to action for individuals to engage deeply with their personal and professional growth, leveraging every available resource to forge a better future.

Imagine a world where your birth status is merely a starting point, not a permanent marker of your life's potential. In this world, your ambitions, talents, and efforts are the true determinants of your social and economic standing. Whether you're an aspiring entrepreneur, a dedicated student, or a professional looking to climb the corporate ladder, the class system presents a landscape ripe with opportunity. Arm yourself with knowledge and skills that are in demand. Education is a powerful equalizer, capable of opening doors to new opportunities and career paths. Seek out opportunities for growth within your career. Networking, mentorship, and continuous skill enhancement are key strategies for upward mobility. Understand and manage your finances wisely. Investment in assets, prudent saving, and wise spending can accelerate your journey up the class ladder. Build your social capital by engaging with your community. Networking can provide support, open new opportunities, and enrich your personal and professional life.

Let me tell you a story. Once upon a time, there was a boy growing up in the woods in a tent. This young boy and his family made daily trips to collect logs for cooking and warmth. This routine, though fraught with danger, provided them with what they needed to survive. Everything changed when the boy befriended another child who introduced him to a different way of living in a log cabin. This encounter highlighted a significant lesson. Sometimes we are limited not by choice but by the knowledge and resources available.

This story teaches us a valuable lesson about life and business—the importance of seeking knowledge and being open to new ways of doing things. Just as the boy learned about log cabins, we too can discover more efficient and sustainable methods to achieve our goals, both personally and professionally.

In life and business, we often inherit practices and beliefs that shape our approach, but it's crucial to question and seek better solutions actively. Blaming others for what we haven't been taught overlooks the reality that people cannot give what they don't possess. Instead, we should focus on acquiring new knowledge and skills. The encounter with the log cabin symbolizes the discovery of more efficient ways to solve problems. Similarly, in business, innovation and efficiency can lead to improved outcomes. Financial growth and personal development are about more than just the resources we have; they're about how we use them and our willingness to learn and adapt. The story underscores the idea that true value and sustainability in life and business come from what we create and leave behind, not from fleeting achievements or possessions.

For example, seeking advice from experts like accountants is essential, but understanding that expertise comes in various forms and learning the language of any field is crucial for true growth. Financial and personal growth require a change in mindset. How we perceive value, resources, and opportunities can significantly affect our success and legacy. Achievements are milestones to share, teaching others that what may seem impossible is attainable with the right knowledge, mindset, and approach.

In essence, this narrative encourages us to explore beyond our current understanding and practices, whether in life or business. By embracing learning, seeking efficiency, and adapting our mindset, we can uncover new paths to success and leave a lasting impact. Elevating your class status is not just a personal victory; it has the potential to uplift those around you. By breaking through social and economic barriers, you become a beacon of hope and inspiration for others. Your success story can encourage future generations to dream bigger and strive harder, fundamentally altering the trajectory of families and communities.

The journey through the class system is one of hope, challenge, and resilience. It's a testament to the human spirit's capacity for growth and transformation. By focusing on increasing one's class through education, professional development, and financial acumen, individuals can rewrite their destinies. This is not just a roadmap; it's a call to action for anyone aspiring to transcend their born circumstances and achieve greatness. In the grand tapestry of human society, your class is not a limitation but a launching pad for your dreams.

<u>You Can Heal</u>

In the realm of personal development, there's a valuable lesson often applied to both life and business: "garbage in, garbage out." This concept underscores the idea that what you consume mentally and emotionally profoundly shapes your personal growth journey. Just as poor input data leads to poor output, the beliefs and ideas you feed your mind impact your overall well-being. This principle forms a fundamental part of the journey to financial wellness, which we'll explore further in "Thriving, In the Black."

Healing the Blame Wound in Life and Business

Life frequently presents challenges, and a lack of fulfillment often signals an area where growth is needed. Many adults find themselves pointing fingers, assigning blame to circumstances, education, or even their upbringing. This common struggle affects both personal lives and ventures in the business world.

Have you ever heard someone say, "My parents never taught me anything about money," or "My parents weren't great with money when I was growing up"? As children, we often perceive our parents as nearly god-like figures with authority and control over our lives, while their imperfections go hidden by our innocence.

However, as we navigate the tumultuous teenage years, our quest for individual identity sharpens our awareness of our parents' flaws. Suddenly, their once-pristine image becomes tarnished by imperfections. Ideally, as we reach adulthood, we embark on a quest for a more balanced view. We start appreciating both their strengths and weaknesses with a newfound sense of perspective and, at times, even a touch of tenderness. But what if we can't let go of that blame, even as adults? What if we keep dwelling on our parents' shortcomings, allowing it to poison our lives? This fixation might stem from genuinely hurtful experiences caused by them or turn into a never-ending cycle of blame, ultimately hurting us more than them.

Let's apply the healing process to both life and business. Just as our bodies can suffer from hidden wounds that slowly drain our physical health, life and business can face similar challenges that affect our financial well-being. These challenges might stay hidden, suffocating our opportunity to grow our income streams. Yet there's a healing process that can be applied to these wounds, resonating with the unconventional spirit of "Thriving, In the Black."

Step 1: Stop the Bleeding (Identify the Problem)

Imagine you have a cut on your hand. The first thing you do is stop the bleeding. In life and business, when things start going awry, it's essential to do the same. Identify what's causing harm, whether it's a toxic blame game or a financial issue, and take immediate action to halt it.

Step 2: Clear the Debris (Deal with Immediate Concerns)

Once the bleeding stops, you're often left with a mess. In both personal and professional spheres, this means dealing with the immediate fallout. It's about crisis management and damage control, tackling urgent issues head-on.

Step 3: Rebuild and Grow (Address the Underlying Issues)

The rebuilding phase in wound healing is when new tissue forms. Similarly, in life and business, it's time to address the root causes of the problem. Develop new strategies, improve processes, and most importantly, grow from the experience.

Step 4: Maturation and Improvement (Adapt and Evolve)

Just as scars take time to fade, real change in life requires patience. During this phase, continually evaluate, adjust, and strengthen your solutions. Adapt and evolve to ensure that old issues don't resurface. This process not only promotes healing but also fosters growth in all aspects of your personal and professional life, turning adversity into opportunities for positive transformation.

It's essential to distinguish reality from myth and kindle the flames of personal growth within. Let's explore some of these common misconceptions.

Myth 1: Money is the Root of All Evil

You've undoubtedly encountered the age-old saying that money is the root of all evil. However, it's time to dispel this myth. Money itself is neither good nor evil; it's a tool, a means to achieve your goals. How you use money determines its influence on your life. In both personal and business contexts, viewing money as a resource for growth and positive impact can shift your perspective. Embrace the idea that growing your financial resources empowers you to achieve more, provide for your loved ones, and make a difference in the world.

Myth 2: Business is Only for the Experts

You may have heard that the world of business is reserved for experts with years of experience. While expertise is valuable, every business journey starts with a single step. Businesses, whether large or small, often begin with a simple idea and a willingness to learn. Being teachable is your most valuable asset. Embrace the fact that knowledge can be acquired, guidance sought, and skills continuously developed. In the realm of investments, opportunities await both beginners and seasoned experts. Embrace your status as a novice, as it marks the initial step towards growth.

Myth 3: Lukewarm is Safe

The allure of staying within your comfort zone in the lukewarm waters of life can be tempting. However, the truth is that lukewarmness rarely leads to significant growth. Life and business thrive on passion, courage, and well-calculated risks. It's better to be either fully committed or deliberately taking a step back rather than remaining in a state of lukewarm indecision. Lukewarmness often fosters regrets, missed opportunities, and unrealized potential. Choose to embrace either extreme, and you'll find that life's experiences have a way of dissolving your fears, fortifying your courage, and banishing procrastination.

Myth 4: Life and Work are Separate Realms

Many people perceive life and work as separate compartments, but in reality, they are interconnected. Your personal journey is intertwined with your professional one and vice versa. The skills honed in one domain often seamlessly transfer to the other. Consider life as a personal venture and business as a life endeavor. Applying business principles such as planning, adaptability, and strategic thinking to your personal life can unlock a newfound sense of purpose and vitality.

Your personal growth hinges on the quality of input you receive. By dispelling these myths and embracing growth, you can navigate both life and work with a clearer perspective and greater purpose.

Picture yourself stepping into the role of CEO of your very own company named "YOU Enterprises." In this company, you get to make all the decisions to shape every part of your organization to strengthen your company for a successful future. Welcome to "YOU." You are the star and cornerstone of this adventure. Your journey begins and ends with you. You hold the keys to your growth and success. Just like proprietary information in a thriving company, your unique blend of talents, skills, and aspirations sets you apart.

Every successful company has something that distinguishes itself in the market. As you stand out with your talents, dreams, and goals, take a moment to answer a very important question. What truly matters to you? Is it family, wealth, health, the environment, time, travel, possessions, education, well-being, contributing to others, recognition, or perhaps the pursuit of freedom? This soul-searching holds the key to your future.

Investing in yourself and nurturing your learning process helps lay the groundwork for a prosperous future. Much like a savvy entrepreneur who carefully manages expenses, consider avoiding unnecessary expenditures, debts, and credit card payments. Think of these as the financial components that help run your personal enterprise. Just as a streamlined business operates efficiently, managing your financial affairs judiciously ensures that your life's journey remains worry-free.

At "YOU," prioritize understanding the difference between being caught up in "Busyness" and striving for productivity in what we refer to as "Business." The concept of Busyness revolves around filling your day with countless activities, yet they may not always help you realize your goals. It's like running on a hedonic treadmill, continuously using your energy without making progress.

Being productive, on the other hand, means focusing on the tasks and actions that move you closer to your goals. Imagine it as taking deliberate steps towards your destination. Now, let's draw a parallel to your financial journey. Just like investing resources into things that take you away from your growth, spreading yourself too thin on nonessential activities takes you away from your personal growth. Using your resources wisely, like saving and investing in sound future endeavors, will help you amplify your returns and growth potential.

Always keep in mind you have the power inside "YOU" to shape and recreate your life. Just like a successful business owner, you can make smart decisions and investments that will bring you a deep sense of fulfillment and joy. As you begin your transformation process, more opportunities will find "YOU," and your enterprise will thrive.

You are invited to embark on this exhilarating adventure of mastering your personal finances and creating a healthier "YOU." You're the CEO of your own life, and the gateway to your greatest prospects lies in comprehending the art of productivity, making sound financial decisions, and investing in the exceptional asset that is YOU. I'm absolutely delighted to work together on this voyage of personal and professional elevation. As we explore the timeless principles and strategic insights within "Thriving, In the Black," you are encouraged to infuse the air around you with the essence of your dreams and aspirations as we venture into your unique journey.

CHAPTER TWO

The Power of Financial Affirmations

Ever doubt your financial abilities? You're not alone! We've all felt uncertain about our money skills. But there's a simple and powerful tool that can change everything. You're here to take control of your financial life, and you're in the right place. Let's start by acknowledging something important: everyone has moments of doubt when it comes to money. It's perfectly normal, even for financial experts.

Let's take a moment to acknowledge your journey. Maybe you've faced financial setbacks, struggled to make ends meet, or just want to boost your financial confidence. Whatever brought you here, know that you're not alone. Many of us have been through the money roller-coaster, and it's okay. Don't worry about financial affirmations; this isn't some new-age hocus-pocus. It's a simple but incredibly effective tool that can reshape your financial reality.

Here's the deal: your thoughts and beliefs about money have a powerful influence on your financial outcomes. If you constantly tell yourself that you're bad with money or that you'll never get ahead, guess what? Your brain believes it, and it becomes your reality.

Financial affirmations are like little positive pep talks for your mind. They're short, simple statements designed to change your money mindset. By repeating these affirmations regularly, you can start reprogramming your brain for financial success and abundance.

What's in It for You?

Let's talk about the benefits. Why bother with financial affirmations, you ask? Well, affirmations help you silence those inner money critics. They replace self-doubt with self-assuredness, giving you the confidence to make better financial decisions. When you focus on positive statements about your financial future, you gain clarity about your goals. You'll be more motivated to save, invest, and work toward those dreams. Imagine saying, "I am financially free," and feeling it. Affirmations can reduce money-related stress and bring a sense of calm to your financial life. Positivity attracts positivity. By embracing financial affirmations, you can start attracting more financial opportunities and abundance into your life.

Our Most Precious Resource

Within our collective existence, there exists a commonplace phenomenon. These seemingly routine behaviors, driven by convenience or oversight, carry significant ramifications. Let's peel back the layers and explore the significance of our choices, particularly regarding water—a renewable yet limited resource that sustains all life on Earth. Water, the essence of existence, flows through our lives in an intricate dance with nature. It's a resource we can find, purify, and package, but we cannot replicate. Without water, life as we know it is impossible. The simple act of turning on a faucet connects us to a web of life that spans continents and ecosystems. It's a thread that ties us to every living being, reminding us of our interconnectedness.

Consider the implications of our water usage. Wasting water isn't just about a high utility bill; it's about squandering a life-giving resource. It's about ignoring the privilege of clean water that so many lack. It's about disregarding the fact that by saving water, we're protecting life in all its forms on this blue planet.

Let's not forget food, another essential element woven into the fabric of existence. Food sustains us, nourishes us, and connects us to the Earth. Yet, a significant portion of the food we produce goes to waste. It's a reality that we can't afford to overlook, not just for our own well-being, but for the global community. In a world where hunger coexists with abundance, every morsel of food wasted is a missed opportunity to alleviate suffering. By reducing food waste, we're not only honoring the resources that went into production but also extending a hand to those who are in need. Our choices reverberate beyond our plates, affecting lives across borders.

Now you might wonder, what does all this have to do with love? The connection is profound. Love isn't just an abstract concept; it's a force that drives our actions and decisions. Love is what compels us to care for one another and for our planet. It's what inspires us to be mindful of our choices, even in the seemingly insignificant moments of turning off a tap or finishing a meal. The act of saving water and reducing food waste is an embodiment of love in action. It's a tangible expression of our interconnectedness, a way of showing gratitude for the blessings we have, and a gesture of solidarity with those who lack necessities.

Applying this understanding to our lives unlocks a cascade of benefits. It starts with mindfulness, being aware of the impact of our choices. It's about valuing resources and being intentional about how we use them. As we embrace this mindset, we begin to make choices that align with our values and ripple outward.

On a personal level, conserving water and reducing food waste brings a sense of responsibility and empowerment. It's a way of contributing positively to the planet and our communities. It instills a sense of purpose in our actions, reminding us that even small steps matter. The benefits extend beyond our individual lives. When we collectively make conscious choices, we contribute to a more sustainable world. We ease the burden on ecosystems, conserve resources, and create a legacy of care for future generations. Our actions have the power to shape policies, influence industries, and drive positive change on a global scale.

As we reflect on the journey of conserving water and reducing food waste, we come full circle to the notion of love. Love isn't just about affection between individuals; it's a force that permeates the universe. It's what propels us to care for the Earth and all its inhabitants. Love is a guiding light that shows us the interconnectedness of life, and through our actions, we manifest that love into tangible impact.

Just as our actions with water and food waste ripple through the world, so do the choices we make in pursuing what we love. In the tapestry of our lives, these passions are the threads that create intricate patterns of joy, accomplishment, and connection. But as we embrace what we love, we must also recognize when it's time to release what no longer aligns with our journey. Memories hold both moments of triumph and challenges. Yet, dwelling on the negative aspects only serves to prolong their influence. In a world where possibilities are boundless, it's essential to pivot towards the positive, towards the love that envelops us, and towards the beauty that paints our existence with vibrant hues.

It's in the conscious act of nurturing love and letting go of what doesn't serve us that we unlock the door to personal growth and transformation. This deliberate choice to focus on the positive, to cultivate what we love, and to release what no longer resonates is an act of empowerment. It's a choice to shape our narrative, embracing the joy and love that life has to offer.

Just as the act of saving water and reducing food waste is a step towards a harmonious world, embracing what we love is a step towards a harmonious life. It's about living authentically, aligning with our passions, and resonating with the essence of who we are. As we do so, we ripple positive energy into the universe, touching lives and inspiring others to embrace their own journey of love and growth.

So, let your heart echo with the question, what do you love? Embrace the power of your passions, cherish the beauty around you, and journey towards a life where love is the guiding force. As we navigate this intricate dance between personal evolution and global harmony, remember that love, in all its forms, is the universal language that bridges the gaps and paints the canvas of existence with vibrant, transformative colors.

Your history doesn't define you; you are a tapestry of evolution, growth, and transformation. The stories you tell yourself wield incredible power. Narratives of victimhood or self-doubt can shape your reality if you let them. But if you switch tracks and embrace narratives of empowerment, abundance, and love, your life will shift accordingly. Unleash the keys to success, whether in your personal life, your business endeavors, your relationships, or your parenting journey, by making love your cornerstone. Immerse yourself in the depths of love, and a new horizon emerges. Cast aside limitations and embrace boundless potential. Love dismantles the barriers that hinder financial abundance, health, happiness, and connections. With love as your guide, manifestations become almost instantaneous. You radiate positivity, inviting opportunities and abundance into your life. A touch of your presence is transformative, dissolving negativity in its wake. Your energy soars, and you become a beacon of well-being.

Picture a world where your heart flutters with boundless enthusiasm. A world where every interaction, relationship, and endeavor is infused with the power of love. Your touch is transformative; your spirit, unbreakable. Love empowers you to accomplish feats that seemed unattainable. You stand invincible, capable of turning dreams into reality. Dive into this love-infused realm across all domains. In relationships, let love be your guide, deepening connections and fostering growth. In your career, infuse every task with passion and watch your impact amplify. In your role as a parent, let love fuel your interactions and see the beauty of growth in your children. When love becomes your driving force, limitations crumble, and the universe aligns with your desires. You become a conductor of joy, fulfillment, and prosperity. Each interaction, venture, and pursuit takes on new dimensions, all underpinned by love's transformative energy.

So, the challenge is to simply fall in love with yourself and life. Tap into the reservoir of love that resides within you—a wellspring that knows no bounds. Allow love to guide your journey, and you'll witness extraordinary shifts in your reality. Your desires will be drawn towards you like a magnet to steel. You'll glide through life with a lightness of being, unburdened by constraints. With love as your ally, success becomes not just a possibility but a certainty. You hold the keys to unlock a life brimming with joy, accomplishment, and satisfaction. The power is within your grasp—the power of love. So, take the plunge and let the currents of love guide you to a world where every endeavor, be it personal or professional, thrives with boundless potential. The transformation begins with you, and the magic of love as your guide.

Love in Life and Business

Throughout the ages, sages and wise souls have whispered a simple yet profound truth: love is the answer. This wisdom transcends time, inviting us to embrace its essence and wield its power in both our personal lives and business endeavors. Love is the foundation on which happiness, success, and fulfillment are built. It's not just about kindness; it's about recognizing the incredible potential it holds to shape our realities.

In partnerships, particularly in marriage, and on the journey of parenting, love becomes the compass guiding us towards an extraordinary existence. By channeling acts of kindness, encouragement, support, and gratitude towards our loved ones, we initiate a powerful cycle. The love we give multiplies and returns to us in ways we couldn't imagine, touching every corner of our lives. It's a ripple effect that influences our health, finances, happiness, and career positively.

Conversely, negativity and harmful emotions manifest as potent energies. Criticism, anger, impatience, and the like resonate in ways that attract further negativity, which in turn infiltrates various aspects of our lives. The law of attraction is at play, amplifying the energy we emit. Therefore, fostering positivity and love in our interactions becomes not just a choice but a necessity. A harmonious environment is created through nurturing positive energy.

Remember, what we extend to others shapes our reality. The power of love, kindness, and empathy is transformative. By weaving these qualities into our partnerships and parenting journey, we create a tapestry of abundance and harmony. But what if relationships feel challenging? The energy we've invested in them often mirrors the energy we've given. A thriving relationship reflects the love, gratitude, and positivity channeled towards it. On the flip side, difficulties can arise when negativity overshadows the love we offer.

It's important to note that relationships aren't solely determined by external factors. The quality of a relationship isn't solely about the other person's actions; it's about the energy we give and how we choose to feel. True transformation occurs when we focus on the positive attributes of our loved ones, nurturing the aspects we appreciate and love. To take charge of our relationships, we tap into the immense power of love. By genuinely seeking out qualities that resonate, we create a shift. It might seem as if the other person is changing, but it's our own transformational energy that's at play, dismantling negativity. However, love doesn't mean forfeiting self-worth or imposing control. It's not about changing someone to fit our preferences. Love respects individuality and boundaries, while also demanding respect for oneself. Love is transformative and resilient, not weak. It thrives when we align ourselves with positive feelings, enabling us to navigate challenges with grace.

In a world rich with diverse relationships, friendships, partnerships, and parenthood, we hold the power to choose what resonates with us. We needn't force affection or invest negativity in what doesn't align. We honor each person's journey, embracing their diversity. Our path is to radiate love and understanding, attracting like-minded souls. As we cultivate our own happiness, the law of attraction draws those who share our energy. So, let love be your guide.

Your Financial Blueprint

In "Thriving, In the Black," we'll dive into your Financial Blueprint, something that has been silently shaping your financial life. Understand that your current financial situation isn't entirely your fault. It's not about blame; it's about understanding. We all have a financial blueprint shaped by our past experiences and family upbringing. This blueprint is like a hidden set of rules and beliefs that guide our money decisions, often without us even realizing it.

Think of your past financial experiences as different enterprises. Some were successful, while others might have struggled. These enterprises, big or small, have left their mark on your financial blueprint. Maybe you had a business venture that failed or invested in something that didn't pan out. These experiences can create limiting beliefs or financial fears that affect your present choices.

Let's introduce a concept that's all about your FUN SCORE. This score reflects how much fun you're having with your finances. If it's low, it means you're not enjoying your financial journey, and it's time for an upgrade. If it's high, great job! You're on the right track.

To change your financial blueprint, you need a target, a destination to aim for. Enter your FUN GOAL. This is your vision for a financially fulfilling life. It's not just about numbers; it's about what truly makes you happy. Do you want to travel the world, buy a dream home, or retire comfortably? Your FUN GOAL is unique to you.

Why Rewire Your Financial Blueprint?

Why should you bother rewiring your financial blueprint? Here are a few fantastic reasons:

Breaking Limiting Beliefs: By understanding and reshaping your financial blueprint, you can break free from those limiting beliefs that have been holding you back.

Informed Decisions: When you know why you make certain money choices, you can make more informed decisions that align with your FUN GOAL.

Increased Financial Confidence: As you gain control over your financial blueprint, your financial confidence will soar. You'll trust yourself more and make choices that empower your financial future.

Boost Your FUN SCORE: The ultimate goal is to boost your FUN SCORE. When you enjoy managing your money, it becomes less of a chore and more of a rewarding journey.

In the upcoming chapters, we'll delve even deeper into how to rewrite your financial blueprint. We'll provide practical exercises and insights to help you transform your relationship with money.

Remember, this journey is about understanding, not blame. Your financial blueprint might have been set in motion by your past, but you have the power to redesign it. Let's start creating a blueprint that aligns with your FUN GOAL and paves the way for financial success and happiness.

Forgiving Financial Mistakes

Let's talk about forgiving financial mistakes. Yes, you heard it right. We're talking about making peace with your financial past. But before we get into the nitty-gritty, here's something important: you're not alone. Let's start by acknowledging that everyone, and I mean everyone, makes financial mistakes at some point. It's like a rite of passage in the world of money. Maybe you overspent on that vacation, invested in a questionable scheme, or just didn't save when you should have. We've all been there, and it's perfectly normal.

Let's tap into some wisdom that transcends personal relationships. Forgiving others, whether it's a friend for letting you down or, perhaps more importantly, forgiving yourself for past financial missteps, is truly liberating. So, why bother forgiving financial mistakes? It's all about releasing the heavy baggage of guilt and shame that often comes with those slip-ups. When you carry that burden, it affects your present and future financial decisions. You might avoid taking calculated risks or shy away from investing because you fear making another mistake.

Forgiving yourself means shedding the guilt and shame that have been holding you back. It's like removing a weight from your shoulders, allowing you to move forward with confidence. When you're not haunted by past mistakes, you can make better financial decisions. You'll be more open to taking calculated risks and exploring opportunities for growth. Forgiveness is like hitting the reset button on your financial life. It paves the way for a healthier, more positive financial future, free from the constraints of the past. Forgiving yourself fosters self-compassion, an essential trait for financial well-being. You'll learn to treat yourself kindly, even when you stumble.

In the upcoming chapters, we'll delve into practical exercises and strategies to help you forgive and move forward. It's all about creating a financial environment that supports your growth and prosperity. Remember, you're not defined by your past mistakes. They're just steppingstones on your journey to financial well-being. So, let's start forgiving and make room for a brighter financial future.

Financial Self-Love and Self-Care

In this chapter, we're diving into something that might sound a bit unusual in the context of finance: self-love and self-care. Yes, we're talking about treating yourself kindly when it comes to money. Before we go any further, let's start with a validation: it's okay to focus on self-love in your financial journey.

First things first, you deserve love and care, especially from yourself. In fact, it's essential in your financial journey. Sometimes, we get so wrapped up in budgets, bills, and investments that we forget the most critical aspect of the equation: ourselves. Let's talk about nurturing a loving relationship with yourself in the financial realm. What does that mean exactly? Well, it's about treating your financial self with kindness, understanding, and patience—just like you'd do for a dear friend.

One of the immediate benefits of financial self-love and self-care is the impact it has on your spending habits and financial decisions. When you truly care about your financial well-being, you're more likely to make mindful choices. For instance, instead of impulse buying, you might pause and ask yourself if the purchase aligns with your FUN GOAL (remember that!). You'll be more attuned to your needs and wants, which can lead to more responsible spending.

Now, here's the exciting part: financial self-love and self-care can open the door to increased abundance. When you treat yourself kindly, you send a powerful message to the universe that you're deserving of financial prosperity. This positive energy can attract more opportunities for wealth into your life.

Let's sum up the benefits of embracing financial self-love and self-care:

Mindful Spending: With mindful spending habits, you'll make more conscious choices about where your money goes, ensuring it aligns with your financial goals.

Reduced Stress: By caring for your financial self, you'll reduce money-related stress and anxiety. It's like a soothing balm for your financial worries.

Increased Abundance: The universe tends to favor those who believe in their own worthiness. Financial self-love can attract more financial abundance and opportunities your way.

Improved Relationships: When you treat yourself with love and care, it often spills over into your relationships with others. You'll find yourself more understanding and compassionate in financial discussions.

We'll delve into practical ways to practice financial self-love and self-care. It's not about extravagance; it's about nurturing your financial well-being from a place of love. Practice asking yourself, "Do I want or need this item? Is buying this item going to bring me closer to any good?" Remember, you're your own biggest financial asset. So, let's take care of that asset and watch it grow.

Breaking the Chains

Today, we're diving into a topic that impacts every aspect of our lives: learned behavior and mindset. These are the silent architects of our existence, shaping not only our individual lives but also casting a profound influence on our relationships and the future of our children. These are the invisible strings that can either hold us back or propel us forward, whether in our personal lives or in the world of business.

"The chains of habit are too light to be felt until they are too heavy to be broken."

-Warren Buffett

First, let's talk about learned behavior. From our earliest days, we're like sponges, absorbing the behaviors, values, and beliefs of those around us. We learn from our parents, family, friends, and the society we grow up in. Some of these learned behaviors serve us well, while others can be like an anchor, holding us back. The way we've learned to approach life and business doesn't just stay with us. It trickles down into our relationships and shapes the world we create for our children. Some of these behaviors and habits are great, like saying "please" and "thank you." Others, not so much.

Ever find yourself reacting to a situation in a way that feels automatic? That's learned behavior in action. It's the stuff we've absorbed over the years, and sometimes, it doesn't serve us well. But here's the good news: you can unlearn those behaviors that hold you back and replace them with more positive ones.

In your own life, learned behavior and mindset dictate your decisions, reactions, and choices. Ever catch yourself saying or doing something and think, "Where did that come from?" That's your learned behavior in action. It can either empower you to achieve your goals or keep you stuck in patterns that no longer serve you. For instance, if you grew up in a household where money was always tight and the mindset was one of scarcity, you might find yourself hesitant to invest in your own business or take calculated financial risks. This can impact your career growth, financial stability, and overall sense of well-being.

Let's talk about how this all spills into other parts of life. When you bring your learned behavior and mindset into a relationship, it becomes a shared experience. If you've got a scarcity mindset, it can create tension around finances, decision-making, and even your ability to plan together. The beliefs and behaviors you each bring into the partnership can either strengthen it or strain it.

Let's imagine the effects on children. They are like sponges too, absorbing everything around them. Your learned behavior and mindset become the foundation upon which they build their own worldviews. If they grow up seeing a healthy balance of ambition, financial responsibility, and resilience, they're more likely to carry those traits into their adult lives. But if they witness a mindset of lack, financial instability, or patterns of behavior that don't serve their best interests, it can set them on a challenging path. The cycle can be repeated, and the torch of learned behavior can be passed on yet again.

Here's the bottom line: learned behavior and mindset aren't just personal matters. They ripple through every aspect of your life, affecting your decisions, your relationships, and the future of your children. The good news? You have the power to reshape this narrative, break free from limiting beliefs, and create a legacy of abundance, empowerment, and resilience for yourself and those you hold dear.

Have you ever caught yourself thinking, "There's not enough to go around" or "I'll never have enough money to do what I want"? That's scarcity thinking at play. It's like living in a world where the glass is always half empty. A lack of mindset can seriously impact your decisions in both life and business. It can make you overly cautious, hesitant to take risks, and resistant to change. But guess what? You can shift that mindset to one of abundance. There's plenty out there for everyone, and you have the power to grab your share.

Are you in a debt loop? Those tricky financial cycles often revolve around events like Christmas, birthdays, and anniversaries. You know the drill: you overspend during the holidays or on special occasions, racking up debt that lingers long after the festivities are over. It's a tough spot, and many of us have been there. But the thing is, these debt loops don't just affect our bank accounts; they affect our peace of mind and our ability to invest in our future. Breaking free from these cycles is a crucial step in achieving financial stability in both your personal and business life.

Creating a Prosperity Mindset

We're about to explore something truly transformative: creating a prosperity mindset. It's all about shifting your perspective from scarcity to abundance and unlocking a world of financial opportunities. And here's the validation you need right now: you absolutely have the power to cultivate this mindset. YOU can do it! No matter where you are in your financial journey, you can nurture a prosperity mindset.

Let's explore some valuable principles. These principles of self-worth and self-acceptance, often associated with personal development, can seamlessly integrate into your financial life. They serve as the secret sauce for building a prosperity mindset.

- Shifting from Scarcity to Abundance: At its core, a prosperity mindset is about changing the way you perceive wealth. Instead of dwelling on what you lack or what you fear losing, it's about recognizing the abundance that surrounds you. It's seeing opportunities instead of obstacles.
- The Power of Belief: What you believe about your financial future can shape your reality. If you constantly tell yourself that you'll never have enough money or that financial success is reserved for others, you're limiting your potential. On the flip side, if you believe in your ability to attract abundance, you're setting the stage for greater financial achievements.

Why Embrace a Prosperity Mindset?

- Increased Financial Confidence: Believing in your ability to attract abundance boosts your financial confidence. You'll be more willing to take calculated risks and pursue opportunities.

- Resilience: With a prosperity mindset, setbacks are seen as temporary hurdles, not insurmountable barriers. You'll bounce back quicker from financial challenges.
- Better Financial Decisions: You'll make financial decisions from a place of abundance, not fear. This can lead to better choices and increased financial success.
- Opportunity Attraction: Abundance attracts abundance. When you focus on prosperity, you're more likely to spot and seize financial opportunities.

We will dive deeper into practical strategies for cultivating a prosperity mindset. It's a journey that can transform your relationship with money and open doors you never thought possible. Remember, you have the power to change your mindset and shape your financial destiny. So, let's get started on this exciting journey to abundance.

Long-Term Value

Let's meet Jim. Jim was a seasoned professional in the world of life insurance. His journey began years ago when he stumbled into the insurance industry almost by accident. Fresh out of college, he took a job at a small insurance firm to make ends meet. Little did he know, this would be the start of a lifelong passion. He also happened to be the top dog in the military when it came to insurance sales. Jim was single-handedly responsible for almost half of the military's insurance policies. One day, his bosses approached him with a puzzled look and said, "Hey, how on earth are you managing to sell all these life insurance policies?"

Jim simply shrugged and replied, "Well, you did hire me to sell life insurance policies, didn't you?" The Colonel paused for a moment, then grinned and said, "Alright, next time, I'm coming with you!" Jim didn't hesitate to agree. He thought to himself, "Well, it's got to be more fun than dealing with my fellow recruiters." So, the Colonel sat in the corner as they set up shop. A soldier walked in, took a seat, and Jim briefly explained the policy to him.

The soldier hesitated and said, "It sounds great, but it costs a bit too much. Plus, I'm being deployed for active duty." Jim nodded and replied, "I get it, times are tough. But here's the kicker: this policy is worth $1,000,000. If, heaven forbid, something were to happen, the military would have to pay your family a cool one million dollars. The guy who just left here just bought it. So, who do you think they'll send to the front lines first?" The room fell silent.

Let's relate this to a common pitfall many of us face: confusing short-term actions with their long-term impact. Imagine going all in at the gym for an exhausting nine-hour marathon, hoping for an instant transformation. The reality, however, is quite different. No matter how intense that one-time effort is, it won't miraculously reshape your physique. Contrast this with a consistent daily workout routine, even if it's just a modest 20 minutes each day. This approach guarantees you'll reach your fitness goals. The only catch? You won't have a precise timetable for your transformation because everyone's journey is unique. Some may see results sooner, while others may progress more gradually. What remains certain is the power of the process, not the timeline.

Our society often pressures us to set rigid deadlines, insisting on results by the end of a quarter, a year, or some arbitrary timeframe. But here's the hard truth: you can't always control precisely when success will knock at your door. The important lesson is learning to be comfortable with this unpredictability. Embrace the idea that, if you adhere to a well-crafted process, success is an inevitable outcome. Whether you're embarking on personal growth or pursuing business objectives, trust in this process. Even if you can't dictate the exact moment your goals will be realized, maintain unwavering dedication to your plan.

So, whether you're striving for personal excellence or aiming for business success, remember this: value is a long-term endeavor. While it's essential to validate your efforts, ensure they're geared toward lasting, sustainable outcomes. Don't let short-term setbacks or the uncertainty of timing discourage you. Have faith in your process, stay committed, and watch as your efforts bear fruit in due course.

Practical Financial Healing Techniques

In this chapter, practical strategies for managing money, budgeting, saving, and investing are intertwined with the holistic approach discussed earlier. The focus is on aligning financial actions with newfound positive beliefs and attitudes.

To embark on a journey of financial healing, one must first establish a solid foundation. This involves assessing the current financial situation, including income, expenses, debts, and assets. Setting clear financial goals, both short-term and long-term, is crucial as well. The aim is to create a roadmap for achieving financial well-being. Budgeting is an essential tool for managing money effectively. It's not about restriction; it's about awareness and control. Creating a budget involves tracking expenses, categorizing them, and allocating funds accordingly. By doing so, individuals can ensure that their spending aligns with their financial goals and values. Saving money is a key component of financial healing. It provides a safety net for unexpected expenses and paves the way for future investments and wealth-building.

Unearthing Genuine Wealth and Joy

Greetings, cherished friends. Today, let's dive into a heartfelt discussion on a topic of immense importance: money. While money is undeniably crucial for daily life, it's vital not to let it become the sole definition of existence.

Let's acknowledge that although money can enhance comfort, offer experiences, and provide a sense of security, it falls short in acquiring life's most valuable treasures. It can't create true moments of happiness, foster profound friendships, or replace the warmth of family love.

Understanding money's role is pivotal. It's a tool that enables a fuller life, yet it should never dominate our purpose. As the journey through financial terrain unfolds, remember that genuine happiness and fulfillment arise from experiences, relationships, and the memories woven.

Learning wise money management from an early stage is essential. Begin by saving for the future, setting achievable financial goals, and diligently working to realize them. Consider each purchase thoughtfully, focusing on items that genuinely matter and contribute to well-being. While planning for the future is crucial, savoring the present is equally vital. Life is fleeting, and every instant counts. Seek out experiences that bring joy, create enduring memories, and nurture a life enriched with purpose and contentment.

Never forget that self-worth isn't tied to digits in a bank account. Inherent value exists within, regardless of financial status. Embrace the essence of self, treasure uniqueness, and discover happiness along the path traveled.

As progress unfolds, recall that money serves as a means, not an end. It's a tool amplifying life, not controlling identity. Embrace self-love, savor life's beauty, and hold close relationships and experiences of genuine importance.

In conclusion, while journeying through the realms of money and finance, remember that true wealth isn't confined to dollars and cents. Its measure is found in the variety of experiences, the depth of relationships, and the joy discovered in everyday moments. By grasping money's genuine value and its place in our lives, you're empowered to live a life truly enriched and meaningful. Always remember, you are cherished.

Believing in Your Journey

Imagine self-belief as the bedrock upon which your dreams take form. It's the resolute trust you hold in your capacities, potential, and vision. With self-belief, you silence uncertainties and amplify your resolve. Remember, the primary person who must have faith in your dream is you.

Consider stepping out of your comfort zone as your leap of faith. It's natural for others to question or doubt your aspirations, particularly if they defy convention. Resistance might come from unexpected sources, perhaps even those closest to you. At such junctures, your self-belief becomes paramount. Ask yourself, Is the pursuit of financial freedom worth the cost you're paying now? Can you endure the status quo, or is it time for transformation?

Imagine your dream as a fragile blossom. Putting it into words is akin to planting that blossom in the soil of your mind. Daily, read your dream as if it's a promise to yourself. Envision it; let it be your impetus. Share it with someone who has faith in you, whose optimism fuels your passion. And bear in mind, every stride you take, irrespective of its size, brings you closer to that dream.

Picture this. The clock ticks, and this instant is yours. Not tomorrow, not someday; but right now! Take that initial step, even if it seems minor. Action begets momentum, and momentum evolves into progress. Every step attests to your belief in yourself, a proclamation that your dreams are worth chasing.

So, fellow believer, acknowledge that this chapter is your anthem of self-belief. As you progress, remember that your self-belief is your paramount power. Much like a seed growing into a towering tree, your self-belief nurtures your dreams into reality.

Imagine yourself as the conductor of an orchestra, with your self-belief as the melody setting the tone. As this chapter concludes, stand tall in your conviction. Though the journey might present challenges, with steadfast self-belief, you possess the capacity to surmount any obstacle.

Now, stride forward with assurance, hold your dream close, and embark on those steps toward your vision. You're poised to make your mark on the world, propelled by the unwavering belief that anything is attainable when you believe in yourself.

> *"Begin with the end in mind."*
>
> -Dr. Stephen R. Covey

Visualization is a potent technique for turning dreams into reality. It involves mentally and emotionally experiencing your desired outcome as if it has already happened. In the context of financial goals, it means vividly imagining the financial future you aspire to. Intentions are like the rudder that steers your ship toward your desired destination. By setting clear intentions for your financial goals, you're telling the universe what you want to manifest. It's about being specific and unwavering in your commitment to your financial vision.

One practical way to incorporate visualization and intention into your financial journey is by creating a vision board. This is a visual representation of your financial goals and desires. It can include images, words, and symbols that resonate with your aspirations. Affirmations, as discussed earlier, play a significant role in manifesting financial goals. These are positive statements that reinforce your belief in your ability to achieve your financial dreams. By repeating them regularly, you're programming your subconscious mind for success.

While visualization and intention are essential, they must be accompanied by inspired action. It's not enough to simply dream about your financial goals; you must take concrete steps toward them. This chapter explores how to create an action plan that aligns with your intentions and moves you closer to your dreams. One practical way to incorporate visualization and intention into your financial journey is by creating an action board. This visual tool serves as a clear representation of your financial goals and desires while also helping you take purposeful action and boost productivity. Think of it as the perfect marriage between your vision board and your to-do list. Your action board can include a combination of images, words, and symbols that deeply resonate with your aspirations, effectively guiding you to stay on track and work toward achieving your financial objectives.

Additionally, we will discover the science behind manifestation. It's not merely a mystical concept; there's actual research supporting the idea that focused intention and visualization can lead to positive outcomes. By understanding the science, you can effectively apply these principles and practices in your life.

In the subsequent chapters, you will find practical exercises and guidance on how to apply these manifestation techniques to your specific financial goals. Whether it's achieving financial freedom, paying off debts, or building wealth, the power of visualization and intention can be a game-changer in making those dreams a reality.

In the Red: The Journey of Becoming

Picture you and a group of friends getting together for a night out. As the evening unfolds, someone suggests a refreshing idea: going on a vacation. After days of toiling away, pouring your energy into work and other commitments, the burden has grown heavier. But then, amidst the chatter and camaraderie, a glimmer of inspiration emerges. It's the suggestion that changes the atmosphere—a collective decision to free yourselves from the day-to-day and indulge in a much-needed getaway. The proposal is met with nods of agreement and spirited cheers. This idea stands out as a beacon of hope, a chance to escape the routine and venture into uncharted territory.

Then, their attention shifts toward you. Their eyes sparkle with anticipation, and their smiles radiate warmth as they reach out to you, their arms extended in an inviting gesture. "Join us!" they exclaim, their camaraderie acting like a magnetic pull. The prospect of embarking on this journey together, creating lasting memories with friends, is simply irresistible. It was an offer you couldn't possibly turn down, as the allure of adventure and shared experiences tugged at your senses.

The next step is choosing the destination, a task that sparks spirited debates and lively conversations. Eventually, a consensus is reached, and the excitement grows as plans take shape. Flights, accommodations, and itineraries become the topics of discussion.

You all scour travel websites, looking for the perfect flight package that will transport you to a land of new experiences.

As luck would have it, a recent credit card acquisition turns out to be a fortunate turn of events. With your bank account on life support and your annual vacation days exhausted, the newfound credit provides a glimmer of possibility. The hesitation wavers as your friends encourage you, "You deserve it. You've worked so hard." The decision is made. Bags are packed, passports secured, and anticipation reaches its peak.

Think back on that instant right after you've hit that "Purchase" button. We've all experienced it. That surge of exhilaration and eager anticipation that accompanies the approach motivation system—you're excited about getting your hands on that new item and the sheer delight of owning something novel and captivating.

Have you ever had that feeling where you make a new purchase, and the excitement is off the charts? It's like déjà vu, right? Then, time passes, and that initial thrill wears off, replaced by a different vibe. Suddenly, out of nowhere, practical worries swoop in, making you question if the purchase was necessary and if it aligns with your financial goals. Budget, upcoming bills, financial plans—all start crowding your thoughts. It's like the excitement dims as these concerns take over. You guessed it. That's good old buyer's remorse, that feeling of regret we've all encountered.

When you step back and look at the bigger picture, it's all about finding that sweet spot between fulfilling your wants and being mindful of your choices. Those times when you pause and think things over, they're just a natural part of the journey. As you ride the waves of emotions after making a purchase, keep in mind that buyer's remorse is a gentle nudge to make decisions wisely. It's a reminder to make choices that not only satisfy your immediate wishes but also keep your long-term financial health in check.

As you stand at the airport gate, surrounded by friends who have become family, a sense of gratitude washes over you. In this moment, the worries of the daily grind seem distant. The promise of new sights, sounds, and experiences beckons, offering a chance to recharge and rejuvenate. The journey ahead is not just a vacation abroad; it is a journey to reclaim a piece of oneself that often gets buried under responsibilities and deadlines. As the plane's engines roar to life, you close your eyes and take a deep breath. The adventure awaits, and you are ready to embrace it fully, knowing that sometimes, the most transformative journeys are the ones that lead you far from the familiar.

You arrive and settle in, ready to plan the weekend's activities. The first adventure is an all-day boat trip. While stepping onto the boat, you consult your map and then inquire, "What's our first destination?" The captain responds with a raspy voice, "Don't worry, just sit back, relax and enjoy ya-self." As you unwind, a quote by Ralph Waldo Emerson comes to mind, "Life is a journey, not a destination." The warmth of the sun, the caress of the breeze, and the mist of the clear blue sea against your skin become vivid sensations as the boat glides across the open water.

The air is electric with excitement as the captain brings the boat to a halt, drops the anchor, and switches off the engine. You gather your snorkeling gear—mask, fins, and snorkel—to prepare for the dive into the deep blue. As you slip into the water, the world above starts to fade, giving way to the mesmerizing underwater world beneath the waves. It's like entering an entirely new dimension, a realm where gravity behaves uniquely, and each movement becomes a graceful dance in slow motion.

You're surrounded by an orchestra of colors, corals painting the seabed, and schools of fish darting by in flashes of silver and gold. Yet, among all the breathtaking sights, there's one creature that catches your eye—a lobster. Crawling along the ocean floor, this lobster is a master of movement. It uses its powerful walking legs to navigate, and its tail, well, that's the secret weapon. It contracts and retracts its tail, propelling itself gracefully through the water with a flicker of finesse. It's like watching a skilled dancer choreograph a mesmerizing routine, all in perfect harmony with the underwater world.

But that's not all. As you continue to explore, you notice something else: lobster larvae. These tiny beings are still in the early stages of their journey. They haven't yet settled on the ocean floor, so they float, almost like little dreams carried by the currents. They're a reminder of the delicate balance of life beneath the surface, a world where even the tiniest creatures have a role to play.

In this underwater wonderland, you're an observer, a guest in a realm where nature's beauty unfolds in ways you've never imagined. It's a world that invites you to slow down, to embrace the quiet wonder of the sea, and to witness the intricate dance of life that thrives beneath the waves. As you resurface and return to the boat, you carry with you a memory of that lobster's graceful dance and the sight of those drifting larvae. It's a story from the depths, a tale of a world that continues to amaze and inspire, just waiting for you to dive in and explore its secrets.

Think about lobsters for a moment. They're fascinating creatures. Inside their tough, armored, unyielding shells lives a soft, vulnerable animal. Lobsters can live to be 100 years old and continue to grow throughout their lifetime. But here's the twist: the rigid shell can't expand. You may be wondering, how on earth does the lobster grow then?

As the lobster continues to grow, its shell starts feeling incredibly confining. Imagine wearing shoes that are too tight; it's uncomfortable and limiting. So, what does the lobster do? It seeks refuge under the shelter of a rock, keeping itself safe from predators. There, it sheds its old shell and begins creating a new one. This process happens multiple times throughout the lobster's life. Each time it outgrows its shell, it feels discomfort and seeks protection under a rock. It's like a signal from within, telling the lobster that it's time to change and grow. Interestingly, if lobsters had an easy way out, like a quick fix to soothe their discomfort, they would never experience growth. They'd remain the same size forever.

Just think about it: when the lobster feels uncomfortable, it goes through this natural cycle of change. It faces adversity head-on, and that's what propels its growth. Similarly, in our lives, times of stress and discomfort can be signals that we're on the cusp of something bigger. They're opportunities for growth, lessons to be learned, and chances to become stronger. So, the next time you find yourself facing challenges or feeling uncomfortable, remember the lobster's journey. Embrace those moments as opportunities to evolve and flourish. Just as the lobster uses adversity to its advantage, you can use your experiences to grow and thrive.

Inside the shell, there is a false sense of security and familiarity. Everything seems stable, and there might be a sense of contentment. However, this comfort comes at the cost of potential growth and innovation. As time passes, the world outside the shell keeps evolving, and new ideas, technologies, and opportunities emerge. Unfortunately, those within the shell remain shielded from these developments, leading to missed chances for improvement and advancement. Breaking free from your shell is essential for any individual or business seeking continuous growth and success. It requires a willingness to embrace change, to adapt to new circumstances, and to step outside of the comfort zone. Just like a shell can burst, breaking free from the metaphorical shell involves confronting fears, taking risks, and being open to learning and growing.

The shell represents self-distortion, where we may persuade ourselves into believing things that may not be true. Without realizing it, we often find ourselves trapped in our own mental shells, where blame, anger, and isolation reside. But outside the shell is where hope, love, and understanding can be found. Since birth, we often live in a shell, swaddled, protected, and confined to our limited perspective. As we grow up, we may still find ourselves mentally stuck in our own shells, limiting our potential and blaming others for our circumstances.

To unlock our full potential, we must focus intently on our goals and take charge of our feelings and actions. Being in the shell leads to blaming others and making excuses, preventing us from realizing the life we truly desire. However, when we step out of our shell, we become more powerful and capable of achieving anything we want. Let's dive into the sea with our lobster friend. Picture this little guy, feeling squished and uncomfortable in his shell. But here's where the magic happens: it takes a bold step, sheds its old skin, and emerges stronger than ever. Just like you, tackling challenges head-on, shedding old habits, and transforming into an unstoppable force. Embarking on this transformative journey is much like the lobster's trying to get out of its shell. It's a powerful analogy for both personal and professional growth, encapsulating the essence of breaking free from limitations, embracing change, and pursuing new opportunities.

Picture yourself in the lobster's shoes, or rather, in its shell. Just as the lobster recognizes the constraints of its shell and decides to embark on the laborious process of removing its shell, you too can acknowledge the limitations that might be holding you back. It's about realizing that growth requires shedding old habits, outdated beliefs, and comfortable routines that no longer serve your greater purpose.

This journey isn't just about discarding the old; it's about actively seeking new opportunities and experiences. Just as the lobster ventures into the open sea to explore uncharted territories, you too must venture beyond your comfort zone. It's in these uncharted waters that you find the chance to learn, evolve, and discover aspects of yourself or your business that you never knew existed.

But let's not forget the pivotal first step in this process: making the time. As Stephen R. Covey wisely put it, "To begin with the end in mind means to start with a clear understanding of your destination." This means knowing where you're headed so you can assess your current position and ensure that every step you take aligns with your desired direction.

So, picture this journey as a dual transformation: just like the lobster shedding its shell and venturing into new waters, you're shedding limiting beliefs and embracing growth. It's a journey of recognizing the shell, daring to break free, and setting forth with purpose and intention. And as you take that first step, remember that the path to growth begins by acknowledging the value of your time and the power of your aspirations.

The Inner Prize

Once at a circus, a very inquisitive young boy approached a balloon vendor with a curious request. He wanted the biggest balloon in the world. The boy asked if different colored balloons would float—red, pink, and even black. The balloon maker, becoming a bit frustrated, explained that balloons rise not because of their colors, but because of what's inside them—the gas and air. That's what propels them to reach new heights.

This simple tale reveals a life lesson that resonates in both personal and business pursuits. Just as balloons soar based on what fills them, success is achieved by what's within us. But here's the thing: if we overinflate the balloons, they can burst and fall. Likewise, our thoughts and emotions fill us up, and if we don't manage this buildup, our actions might explode in unexpected ways. Think about it—our emotions and attitudes shape our decisions and actions. If we let negativity and stress build up unchecked, it can lead to unproductive behavior, just like an overfilled balloon that bursts. Learning to manage our thoughts and emotions is like maintaining the right amount of air in a balloon. It ensures we don't burst with negative behaviors and instead rise towards success.

Let's apply this wisdom to tip the scale of success in life and business. Imagine facing challenges like deadlines or setbacks. If you let stress build up unchecked, it could lead to poor decisions and strained relationships. But if you learn to manage stress, communicate effectively, and approach problems with a positive attitude, you can navigate through difficulties more smoothly. Likewise, in the business world, managing stress, staying adaptable, and maintaining a positive outlook can make all the difference. Just as a balloon needs the right amount of air to rise without bursting, you need to find the balance between emotions and actions to achieve success without burning out.

The tale of the balloons teaches us to manage what's inside us—our emotions and thoughts—just as we manage the air in a balloon. By doing so, we can avoid the explosion of negative behaviors and instead soar to new heights in both our personal lives and our business endeavors. This principle is a lot like squeezing an orange. When you do that, you expect orange juice to come out, right? You'd be surprised if apple juice came out instead. Why? Because whatever's inside is what's going to show up. In the same way, our internal state shapes our external actions and outcomes, both in life and in business. Just like a well-filled balloon or a freshly squeezed orange, managing our inner world can lead us toward the path of success.

Let's think about this in a bigger way. Imagine someone says something that gets under your skin. It's like they're squeezing you, and what comes out? Happiness, sadness, fear, anger—it's like a bunch of emotions spill out. But here's the kicker: what comes out is what's already inside you.

We often say, "Well, I reacted that way because of what they said, did, or didn't do." But truth be told, it's about what's already in you. If you're not happy with what's coming out, guess what? You can actually change it. Besides, why would you want to hand over that much power to any person? Stating another made you angry, hostile, or even happy is the same as stating to the world that you are helpless. This is not true. This is also not what you mean to say. So, take stock of your words and actions.

Just like the oranges we enjoy, it's about what's inside that counts. You can have good stuff inside—positivity, courage, happiness. And you know what? You can change what's inside too. It's like giving credit to the good things in life and being grateful for them. Just enjoy the oranges of your life, and hey, give a little shoutout to the big guy upstairs for the good stuff too.

I've always believed that everyone, regardless of their job title, is in sales. Even if you're not officially labeled as a salesperson, if your work involves interacting with people, then you're in the realm of sales. This idea resonates strongly with the words of Zig Ziglar.

In the world of "Thriving, In the Black," there's a fundamental aspect that showcases your dedication and empathy: the relationships you cultivate with your customers. With every interaction, you engage with individuals who have their own unique needs and concerns and rely on your expertise. It's crucial to recognize the trust they invest in you and the significant impact you have on their choices.

Your commitment to customer-focused engagement, where their needs and satisfaction are at the forefront, is already a remarkable achievement. Your ability to actively listen to their requirements, convey solutions in relatable terms, and provide ongoing support reflects your exceptional approach. But have you thought about what could take your business to the next level? Think about the concept of prospective validation. Just as nurturing relationships is crucial, embracing growth and evolution is essential for "Thriving, In the Black" too. Envision implementing innovative tools and techniques that enhance the customer experience—simplifying processes, reducing complexities, and boosting efficiency. By integrating these forward-thinking strategies, you showcase a steadfast commitment to staying ahead in your field and delivering top-notch service.

Furthermore, your journey towards progress can serve as a guiding light for your family, peers, and colleagues. By showcasing your willingness to embrace change and relentlessly pursue excellence, you foster a culture of motivation and advancement. It's not only about reaching milestones but also about instilling a mindset of continuous learning and development within your team. As you validate the meaningful connections you build with your customers, reflect on how you can elevate your business. The path from good to exceptional involves embracing innovation, nurturing growth, and consistently motivating those you work with. Your dedication lays the foundation; let the pursuit of ongoing improvement propel you toward a future that surpasses even your highest dreams.

Breaking Free from the Past and Committing to the Future

A widespread barrier that hinders numerous individuals from realizing their full potential is their deep attachment to their past selves. This sentiment is frequently voiced as the familiar refrain, "I've always been this way," as people find comfort in their existing situations. However, this mindset can prove restrictive and detrimental. Often, this realization becomes apparent during periods of intense struggle, like moments of crushing defeat and burning adversity.

The essence of becoming a self-made millionaire extends beyond amassing wealth; it signifies a profound self-transformation. Achieving such a milestone requires a radical departure from one's former self, ushering in an entirely new version. This transformation is marked by the development of exceptional qualities that go beyond character—encompassing determination, discipline, decision-making, and strength. These qualities elevate one's individuality and contribute to a more well-rounded and enriched character. Imagine personal transformation as a passage through a doorway. Yet, this door fits only the individual, not their burdens. Many mistakenly attempt to carry the weight of others as they journey forward, driven by a desire to rescue those around them. However, this noble endeavor often leaves them too weak to support themselves.

The true reward of achieving wealth isn't solely rooted in material accumulation; it emerges from profound internal metamorphosis. It involves becoming an improved version of oneself, possessing not only the means to indulge in material comforts but radiating qualities that inspire and uplift others. The journey toward self-made millionaire status entails more than accumulating possessions; it's about transforming into an individual capable of influencing both people and circumstances. In this context, prioritizing self-preservation before assisting others isn't a selfish act; it's a necessity for survival and empowerment. By choosing this path, one becomes an even more valuable contributor to their family and community. This transformation entails shedding preconceptions, self-education, personal growth, and self-improvement, enabling them to eventually uplift those they care about.

The pursuit of success divides individuals into two camps: first, those who seek shortcuts and second, those who wholeheartedly commit to the journey. The majority gravitate toward swift solutions, drawn by the allure of immediate gains. Often influenced by peers sharing a similar mindset, almost all of someone's thinking can be shaped by their social circle. Associating with those who embrace minimal effort and post-work socialization leads to shared behavior and perspectives. Conversely, aligning with high-achieving individuals fosters the absorption of their traits and values, influencing one's own path to excellence.

Ultimately, the choice between mere interest and genuine commitment to goals is a defining juncture. It's a distinction that guides individuals toward lasting transformation or fleeting curiosity. The path to personal growth commences with the acknowledgment that personal commitment serves as the bedrock of enduring success. This commitment elevates aspirations from mere dreams to tangible accomplishments. Ultimately, commitment is the puzzle piece that completes one's goals. It propels intentions into achievements, breathing life into even the loftiest aspirations. Without commitment, promising goals may forever remain unfulfilled aspirations. So, ask yourself: are you merely interested, or are you genuinely committed? Within that commitment lies the strength, resilience, and determination needed to propel your journey to greater heights. Keep in mind, commitment bridges the gap between dreams and reality, transforming goals from possibilities to certainties.

Show Up

All eyes were drawn to a man making his way to the podium, grief palpable in the air. The room seemed to hold its breath, a hushed anticipation settling over the space. Despite the weight of grief he undoubtedly carried, there was a resolute determination in his step.

"I'm sorry for the delay; my wife just passed away," he announced. As an observer, you could sense the mixture of emotions that surrounded him. The room's atmosphere seemed to shift, becoming a blend of empathy, respect, and a shared understanding of the pain he must be feeling. His appearance was marked by a stoic composure, a façade that tried to hide the profound sorrow he was undoubtedly experiencing. His eyes, though holding a hint of weariness, were also filled with a quiet strength.

"Alright, we've got a packed agenda for today, so let's get started," he stated. A gentle voice whispered from the audience, "Are you okay?" He replied, "Well, as you can imagine, the pain is unlike anything I've ever felt, but I've got a lot to accomplish today, so let's continue."

The environment itself seemed to take on a muted quality, as if everyone present recognized the need to tread lightly around his heartache. It was as if space itself acknowledged the depth of his love and the heavy burden he carried. In that moment, as he stood at the podium, the room held a collective breath, ready to listen, support, and be there for him as he addressed the challenges ahead. It was a scene marked by a profound sense of humanity and an unspoken acknowledgment of the love that binds families together in the face of adversity.

Someone asked, "What happened?" He replied, "She died in a car accident." Another asked, "Are you okay?" He answered, "We can't bring the entire nation to a standstill because of this. This topic isn't on today's agenda. Believe me, nothing would please me more than to step back from this podium and cry, but I can't. Why? Because I'm an adult, and I have responsibilities to fulfill. So, let's take one more question regarding my wife, and then we're moving forward."

Someone else asked, "Did you tell your children yet?" He replied, "The children were in the car with their mother at the time of the accident. They are at the hospital; my son is in a coma, and my daughter lost her leg."

This section holds a lesson that resonates deeply: the unyielding power of showing up, even in the face of personal grief and other challenges. The message is clear and echoes in the heart and soul. Amidst his own grieving, he didn't falter. He didn't retreat from his responsibilities or let sorrow shroud his commitment. No, he still showed up for his country, for the task at hand. His resilience became a testament to the strength of the human spirit, a reminder that we can choose to stand strong even when life's waves threaten to knock us down.

And so, as we witness this embodiment of courage, the question remains: Can we show up? Can we rise above our personal battles and stand for the things that matter? Can we show up for our nation, our work, our family, and friends? Can we honor our duties, uphold our promises, and show up for ourselves?

It's an invitation to step into our own strength, to realize that we have the power to overcome adversity and make a difference. Just as he exemplified, showing up isn't always easy, but it's a choice that speaks volumes about our character and our determination.

Life is simple, and consistency is the key. The work you invest in today shapes the outcome you receive tomorrow. If you choose to stay idle, remaining in the sanctuary of your bed or the familiarity of your couch, if you let comfort dictate your decisions and take the easy route, be prepared for the hardships that will inevitably follow.

Yet, if you dare to take the path less traveled, if you rise from your slumber, if you embrace discomfort and relentlessly push yourself beyond the ordinary, you will witness transformative power.

It's essential to remember that what you achieved yesterday holds no sway over today's scoreboard. As dawn breaks, the count resets to zero, and it's your actions now that truly matter. The promotion, the workout, the achievements of yesterday become mere footnotes compared to the journey that lies ahead. Each morning grants you a fresh chance to tackle the day with renewed energy. Reflecting on your efforts is a ritual that pays dividends. At the end of the day, look in the mirror before going to bed. Ask yourself, "Did I give my best today?" If the answer is "yes," that signifies progress. If you consistently pursue this path of incremental improvement, day after day, year after year, you'll find yourself standing amidst a masterpiece of growth.

Let this be a reminder, a rallying call that resonates through every aspect of our lives. Let it be a beacon of inspiration, urging us to be present, to be engaged, and to show up not only when it's convenient but especially when it's challenging. Because in those moments, in those acts of courage, we find our truest selves and become the force of change that we aspire to be.

Remember, it's not about attempting to achieve everything in a single day or week. Instead, it's about the daily pursuit of becoming better, even if it's just a small step forward. Over time, these seemingly insignificant steps coalesce into a journey of profound transformation. So, step out of your comfort zone, embrace the grind, and stay relentless in your pursuit of improvement. The outcome will be a life marked by progress, a canvas painted with the brushstrokes of your commitment and growth.

CHAPTER THREE

Employment & Entrepreneurship

Employment + Entrepreneur + Business = JOB FUN

Life often presents us with a unique difference in that of the employee and the entrepreneur. These distinct roles, jobs, and businesses play pivotal parts in shaping not only our financial landscape but also our interaction with the world around us. As you embark on your journey toward a successful life and thriving business, it's important to understand the key differences and benefits that come with each path. Within "You Enterprises," we'll dissect active work, which demands your time as an employee or in self-employment, and passive work through investments and business ventures. Let's shift our attention to another aspect of your business, your income. The aim is to manage your earnings wisely, with two main objectives: strengthening passive income sources and making progress towards your desired FUN Score and FUN Goal.

Active Income as an employee or a self-employed individual involves direct participation and dedicated time. This income stream stems from your daily endeavors, where your expertise, skills, and time are traded for financial compensation. While this avenue ensures a steady inflow, it's essential to recognize that it often comes hand in hand with limitations on your time and resources.

In homes everywhere, a familiar scene unfolds, one that echoes in the hearts and minds of so many people. A young, newly employed individual rushes inside, clutching their very first paycheck with eager anticipation. The joy on their face is undeniable as they hold the envelope high, their innocence shining through. But there's (reality ahead) a twist waiting to pounce, as a knowing observer playfully asks, "How does it feel, opening that first check?" It's as if they've seen this show before and know the plot inside out.

Tearing into that long-awaited paycheck, the enthusiasm palpable, they confidently discard the envelope with a flourish. With a confident, almost theatrical gesture, they cast the envelope aside. Every line in the document is scrutinized with the precision of a seasoned detective on a high-stakes case. FICA, state and local taxes, and federal income taxes come into focus (and boy, can they add up to a hefty chunk, sometimes devouring as much as forty cents on every hard-earned dollar).

It's as if the universe itself is sharing a hearty chuckle at their expense. A moment of realization dawns, taxes hit twice?! First, they vanish before you even lay hands on your paycheck, and then, they sneak up again when you make a purchase (to the tune of about a dime on every dollar). That's half your income gone before you've even savored that burger and fries. And then, the hopeful smile they wore at the start begins to fade, replaced by a furrowed brow and a sigh that feels like surrender. It's the bitter taste of reality sinking in.

The culprit? Taxes! Frustration sets in, and they reluctantly listen as their parents explain why a significant chunk of their hard-earned money won't make it into their pocket. It's like the moment when the truth about the tooth fairy dawns, and it's just one of many such revelations as they navigate the complexities of the real world. The lesson? "You have to pay taxes for everything," followed by a litany of different types of taxes they'll encounter throughout life. Next in line is the intricate world of interest.

On the other side of the coin lies passive income, the department where your money works for you. It encompasses dividends, royalties, rents, and various investment returns. Here, your role shifts from direct involvement to smart decision-making. It's about putting your money to work in ways that generate financial growth without the need for constant personal effort.

Let's combine these two departments and create a financial masterpiece. Imagine directing 100% of your income toward constructing a robust passive income structure. This strategic approach funnels your earnings into investments, budding businesses, and ventures designed to generate self-sustaining revenue streams. Ultimately, the goal is to boost your FUN (Financially Unrestricted Number) Score and inch closer to your FUN Goal. This figure signifies the threshold where your passive income sustains your lifestyle at a comfortable level, granting you the liberty to pursue endeavors of your choice. Your FUN Goal, then, is the target amount that empowers you to maintain your lifestyle through passive earnings.

Embrace your JOB (Journey of Becoming). Employment isn't inherently negative; it's all about how you perceive it. Think of it as part of your journey, and sometimes we find ourselves at a standstill. You can have a job if you view work simply as a means to earn money. You can have a career if your work is a core part of who you are and your sense of progress. You can have a calling if your work contributes to something greater than yourself. It's like customer service: the difference lies in the number of people you serve. An employee serves one customer, the owner, while an owner serves many customers.

Imagine your future self, standing confidently at the intersection of your dreams and reality. Your eyes are filled with a sparkling determination, reflecting on the journey you've embarked upon. You radiate a quiet strength that comes from overcoming challenges and turning them into steppingstones. Your stride is purposeful, guided by a vision that once seemed distant but now feels within reach. Every setback you encountered has become a lesson, and every triumph a testament to your unwavering spirit. Your future self is a beacon of inspiration, reminding you that every step you take today is a stride towards the greatness you're destined to achieve.

As you navigate the realms of active and passive income, remember that each path has its merits. The stability of active income can provide a foundation, while passive income offers the prospect of financial freedom. By competently dividing your income and wisely deploying it, you can build a world where your earnings multiply, your investments grow, and your dreams come within arm's reach.

The Crucible of Isolation (How to turn Dreams into Reality)

We've all had dreams, those cloud-like aspirations that speak to us in moments of quiet. During our youthful years, we frequently have a lot of dreams. It struck me that the true birthplace of dreams is in isolation. Yes, solitude, that tranquil realm where your thoughts can wander freely, and your dreams can take root. Imagine entering isolation, a cocoon of introspection. It's like a caterpillar seeking refuge within its cocoon, emerging later as a stunning butterfly. Odd, right? Seeking greatness through isolation? It's in these solitary moments that the seeds of transformation are sown.

Isolation isn't about staying on the outskirts; it's about stepping willingly into its embrace. It's a choice to delve deep within, to confront your dreams head-on. Picture it as a self-imposed challenge: no distractions, just you and your thoughts. And believe me, when you eventually emerge, the person you were before won't be the same. You'll emerge stronger, clearer, more focused.

Let's get real for a moment. Isolation isn't about drowning in distractions, numbing your mind with information overload, or stressing over minutiae. It's about discovering strength in simplicity, finding clarity in tranquility. Think of it as a mental gym, where you work out your focus, a boot camp for your mental muscles. Remember, isolation isn't weakness; it's the key to forging mental resilience.

So, here's the deal. While in isolation, don't squander this precious time cluttering your mind. Reject the intrusion of noise and emptiness. Instead, welcome the stillness, relish the silence. Let your thoughts roam freely, unburdened by the perpetual buzz of the outside world. Utilize this period to declutter your mind, refine your focus, and hone your dreams.

Why, you ask? When you finally emerge from isolation, you'll carry an unparalleled clarity. Your vision will be sharper, your goals more crystallized, the nonsense stripped away. And let me tell you, the version of you that exits isolation is primed for greatness.

Remember, isolation is a cocoon of transformation, a sanctuary where dreams flourish, and inner strength is fortified. Embrace the solitude, immerse yourself in your thoughts, and emerge as the butterfly—majestic, potent, and poised to soar. This journey into isolation isn't a retreat; it's a stride toward becoming the best rendition of yourself. But let's not halt our momentum here. As you step out of isolation, armed with newfound clarity and energy, there's a seamless segue into another vital facet of your journey: focus. Are you ready to take the leap? Cherish life and its moments that are woven together. These moments weave our history, our future, and the present into the tapestry of our existence.

While traversing this path, it's crucial to remember that yesterday, with its joys and challenges, has now solidified into history. Tomorrow, holding its blend of unknowns and opportunities, remains shrouded in mystery. However, right at this very instant, within the confines of today, lies a precious gift—the present. Just as isolation serves as a cocoon for transformation, this present moment serves as a platform for focused growth.

The present is where we stand, where we breathe, where we feel the heartbeat of life. It's easy to get lost in the past, to let the weight of regrets or nostalgia overshadow the here and now. Equally tempting is to let worries of the future cloud our vision and steal the beauty of today. But let's pause, take a breath, and look around. In the present, the sun paints the sky with its warm hues, and the breeze whispers secrets through the leaves. Each heartbeat is a reminder of life's rhythm, each smile a testament to the moments that make our souls shine.

In this very instant, we have the power to shape our reality, to make choices that ripple through time. The decisions we make today can become the steppingstones to a future we dream of. The connections we nurture now can bloom into relationships that anchor us. So, let's seize the gift of the present. Let's embrace the beauty of this moment and fill it with purpose, kindness, and gratitude. Let's paint the canvas of our lives with vibrant strokes of love and joy.

As we navigate the ebb and flow of time, let's remember that while yesterday holds lessons and tomorrow offers potential, today—this precious present—is where our hearts beat, where our dreams take root, and where the magic of life unfolds. And just like the transformation that occurs in isolation, the focused growth we achieve in this present moment shapes the future we envision. Let's make the most of today, for it is the greatest gift we'll ever receive.

Because you've only got 24 hours in a day. Sounds like a decent amount, doesn't it? But let's break it down a bit. You spend about 8 hours sleeping, which is crucial for recharging your body and mind. Then, there's the standard 9-to-5 work hours for most people, accounting for another 8 hours. So far, that's 16 hours allocated. Let's factor in the essentials. You need to eat, right? Breakfast, lunch, and dinner, roughly an hour each. That's 3 more hours gone, bringing us to 19 hours utilized. But wait, there's still more to consider. You've got to get ready in the morning, and there's that commute to and from work. Add it up, and we're down to 20 hours.

So, here's the reality: you've got 4 hours left. Four hours of your day to do what matters most to you. That's where the game changes. Those four hours, that's your canvas, your opportunity to craft something extraordinary.

This is where focus steps into the spotlight. Tunnel vision takes over. It's all about having a clear game plan, a vision of where you're headed and who you're aiming to become. Distractions can't be allowed to knock you off course during these crucial hours. Stay vigilant against distractions.

Here's an analogy to help you get it: someone sneaks a pinch of salt into your food. You ask, "Will it be alright?" Of course. But what if that person tosses poison into your meal? Suddenly, you're worried about getting seriously sick, right? Got it. Let's take it up a notch. Picture your arch-enemy sneaking pepper into your food. Once again, you're thinking, "Will things be okay?" They will be. Now, think about your best friend, the one who accidentally spills poison into your dish. What's the situation now? "Well," you might think, "you could end up really ill."

The lesson to learn here is this: every single day, you must act as the guardian of your mental space. Picture it like having your very own mental security system. You decide what's allowed and what's firmly denied entry into your mental territory. It's not about just letting anything slip into your thoughts. Imagine yourself as the protector, only permitting things that genuinely align with and benefit you. And don't forget this: just as you're mindful about what enters your body, be fiercely watchful about what infiltrates your mind. It's your realm, and you're the one in charge.

Now, those four hours are the concentrated essence of your day. It's your time to invest in growth, chase dreams, and stride towards the person you're aiming to become. It's not about staying busy; it's about being genuinely productive. When you're laser-focused during those four hours, incredible things begin to unfold. Goals get nearer, skills get honed, and progress becomes undeniable. It's the contrast between drifting aimlessly through life's currents and steering your own ship confidently towards the destination you've set.

So, as you glance at the clock, remember that time is both your ally and your challenge. Embrace the fact that even within the constraints of 24 hours, you have the power to shape your future. It all boils down to how you wield those four hours of focused dedication, turning them into stepping-stones on your journey to greatness.

The Dual Approach: Integrating Active and Passive Income

Picture this: you've got two income streams flanking you, one on the right and another on the left. Welcome to the Dual-Sided Income approach, a strategy that's all about diversifying your earnings and finding that sweet spot of financial stability.

Let's start with the side on your right, the Strong Side, where your active income resides. This is where most of us hustle, whether it's a 9-to-5 job, freelancing, or side gigs. It's the money that keeps our daily lives rolling, but it demands your most precious resource: time. You give it your all, facing challenges head-on, delivering results, and securing your current lifestyle and financial comfort.

Now, over to the left, the Weak Side, your passive income haven. This is the smart wealth-building zone. It's about investments that work for you, like stocks, real estate, and other avenues that make money even when you're not hustling. Imagine that income rolling in without you constantly grinding. It's like a promise of lasting financial freedom that paves the way for you to choose how you live, not just how you survive.

Balancing both sides for Financial Strength is the real game here. Balancing these sides builds real financial muscle. The goal is to elevate the weak side to be as strong as the active side. It's about acquiring new skills, exploring investment opportunities, and tapping into expert wisdom. By setting up retirement funds, creating passive income streams, and investing wisely, you're crafting a roadmap to a prosperous future.

With determination, we picture a future where passive income not only matches but even outpaces active earnings. This isn't just about stability; it's about unlocking a life where your terms rule. Finding this equilibrium takes commitment, flexibility, and a mindset hungry for growth.

At the end of the day, we embody the art of balancing both sides, active and passive income. By harnessing the strengths of each side, we're sculpting a financially secure future bursting with chances for triumph and fulfillment. It's a journey marked by intention, persistence, and the belief that financial equilibrium isn't a pipe dream but a very attainable reality. Create balance, and craft a life where our money serves us as much as we serve it.

Active vs. Passive Work

Imagine an old man passing down a timeless lesson about life to his grandson. He looks at the young boy and shares, "There's a battle raging within me," he says. "It's a fierce fight between two wolves." He pauses to let the words sink in. One wolf, "In the Red," embodies negativity: anger, envy, sorrow, regret, greed, arrogance, self-pity, guilt, resentment, inferiority, lies, false pride, superiority, and ego. He then shifts his focus. The other wolf, "In the Black," represents positivity: joy, peace, love, hope, serenity, humility, kindness, benevolence, empathy, generosity, truth, compassion, and faith. As you listen to this wisdom, you realize that this battle between two wolves isn't just a tale for the old man and his grandson. It's a battle within you too and within every person. We all carry these contrasting forces within us.

Now, think about how this applies to YOU, Enterprises. Just like the wolves, there's a side within your organization that can be nourished to dominate. One side might be filled with doubts, uncertainties, and hesitations that can hold you back. On the other hand, there's another side within you that's brimming with possibilities, innovations, and ambitions waiting to be unleashed.

Imagine the echo of a young boy's question resounding in your thoughts, "Which wolf will win?" It's a story of two contrasting forces within us, and the answer lies in the actions we take, the choices we make, and the path we decide to nurture. Will you succumb to doubt and negativity, or will you cultivate optimism, growth, and progress?

Let's discuss the little voices in your head. You know the ones. The ones that mold your actions, shape your thoughts, and color your worldview. Think of them as little advisers residing in your brain. One is like a cautious friend, suggesting you stay within your comfort zone, blend in, and question yourself. The other is your personal cheerleader, consistently boosting your self-assurance and spurring you onward. Just as the wolves in our tale symbolize, it's a matter of choosing between nourishing doubt or fostering positivity.

We've all had those moments when the doubting voice takes center stage. It's the one that makes you question if you should share your opinion, stay silent when someone's being offensive, or feel insecure about your abilities. It's fueled by self-doubt and fear of not fitting in. Just like the evil wolf, it thrives on negativity. But then there's the other voice, the one that reminds you of your uniqueness, your value, and your right to be heard. It's the one that says, "You're different, and that's awesome!" This voice doesn't just talk to you; it's talking to everyone else too. And here's the thing: it's time to let your own voice shine through the noise. It's time to let it rise above the doubts and make itself heard. Because when you do that, you're not just empowering yourself; you're inspiring others to do the same. This is like nurturing the good wolf inside you.

Imagine a world where everyone felt confident enough to speak up, where diverse viewpoints were welcomed, and where conversations flowed freely. Believe it or not, it's something you can actively be a part of. By embracing both of your inner voices and letting them be heard, you're contributing to change. You're breaking stereotypes, expanding discussions, and creating an environment where everyone's voice matters.

This isn't just about personal growth; it applies to business too. In a company, a similar dynamic exists. There's the voice of caution that might hold back innovation, and then there's the voice of creativity that propels progress. By embracing both sides of the coin, your businesses can foster a culture of innovation, where every employee's perspective is valued.

Alright, let's get to know that other little voice in your head, the one that's always shouting, "Let's do this!" This voice is like your own personal cheerleader, your source of motivation, and your guide to taking action. It's the one that pushes you to grab opportunities, face challenges head-on, and step out of your cozy comfort zone. This voice is all about firing up your drive, fueling your passions, and transforming your dreams into reality. It's like feeding the good wolf in the story.

The "Go for it!" voice isn't into second-guessing or hesitating; it's all about smashing boundaries. It's the friend who tells you, "Hey, your dreams are worth chasing, no matter what hurdles are in the way." When you lend an ear to this voice, you become unstoppable. It reminds you that you're the boss of your destiny, and you have the steering wheel to navigate your life toward your aspirations.

So, which voice are you going to crank up? Will you let the doubting voice get the megaphone, or will you amplify the "Go for it!" spirit that propels you forward? Embrace your unique outlook, make sure your voice is heard, and cheer others on to do the same. And when that "Go for it!" voice starts speaking up, don't hit mute. Instead, answer its call to action. Embrace challenges, take those calculated risks, and chase after your dreams with unstoppable enthusiasm.

Together, we can change the conversation, dismantle barriers, and build a world where every voice adds to the symphony of change. It's time to quiet down the doubtful voice and let the resounding "Go for it!" echo. You've got the power to transform the world, conquer challenges, and shape a brighter future; it's all within your reach. This spirit applies not just to your personal life but also to businesses. Just as you can amplify your "Go for it!" voice in your individual journey, businesses can foster an atmosphere of boldness and innovation. By embracing risks and pushing boundaries, companies can drive progress and create breakthroughs that change the game.

So, validate your inner cheerleader, give it a nod, and let it lead the way. By following the "Go for it!" call, you're not just embracing change; you're becoming the change you want to see. The power to decide is in your hands. Just as the old man wisely advised, the one you feed will ultimately prevail. Feed the wolf of innovation, ambition, and positive change within YOU, Enterprises. Embrace the values of joy, peace, love, and empathy. The battle within you shapes the path your organization takes. It's your call and your actions that will determine which wolf emerges victorious.

In the confusion that often arises from terms like interest rates, 401(k), Simple IRA, stocks, and real estate, you're not alone in finding these concepts perplexing. It's completely understandable if these terms leave you feeling overwhelmed or even questioning your understanding. But fear not, as you're about to uncover the empowering truth.

Expanding on the benefits of understanding these concepts, consider how knowledge truly is power. While the financial world might seem intentionally convoluted, it's not meant to make you feel inadequate. In fact, Wall Street, banks, and financial professionals might use complex language to create a mystique around their services. However, you have the ability to decode this language and grasp the concepts just as well.

So, if you've ever felt like only experts could navigate the intricacies of finance, here's a revelation: you can do it too. By breaking down these terms, understanding their implications, and demystifying financial jargon, you not only take control of your own financial decisions but also liberate yourself from the unnecessary confusion. After all, financial literacy is not about being a specialist; it's about equipping yourself with the knowledge to make informed choices and secure your financial future.

In the realm of professional endeavors, a prevailing trend has emerged: many individuals dedicate their efforts to work for others, rather than cultivating their own ventures. At YOU, Enterprises, and in the Business of You, we uphold a distinct perspective—one that recognizes our personal enterprises as comprising two vital departments: Active and Passive work.

The Active Department comes into play when you immerse yourself in the operational facets of your business, be it through traditional employment, self-employment, or engaging in a side hustle. On the other hand, the Passive Department is where you invest time and resources in building the foundations of your business, nurturing avenues like a 401(k), Simple IRA, stocks, and real estate.

It's a common occurrence for most of us to channel our energies primarily into Active Work, often relegating the Passive side to the shadows. However, our philosophy is rooted in the belief that true prosperity springs from a harmonious balance between the two. Our aim is to diligently work on both fronts, fostering the growth of the Passive Department until it equals or surpasses the heights achieved by the Active side.

In this story, our greatest goal is to see the harmony of our efforts reach a magnificent peak. We want our Passive work to stand strong alongside, or even surpass, the achievements of the Active work. This balanced teamwork is essential for not only maintaining but also boosting our accomplishments, revealing the full potential of both the "Business of You" and the journey to financial freedom. Don't worry, understanding and keeping track of your net worth doesn't need to be complex. Here's what you need to do:

<u>Make a List of Your Assets: List all the things you own that have value</u>.

Cash in checking and savings accounts

Investments (stocks, bonds, mutual funds)

Retirement accounts (401(k), IRA)

Real estate (home, rental properties)

Vehicles

Valuables (jewelry, art, collectibles)

Calculate the Total Value: Add up the values of all your assets to get the total value of your assets.

List Your Liabilities: Next, make a list of all your liabilities, which are debts you owe to others. Examples include:

Mortgage

Student loans

Car loans

Credit card debt

Personal loans

Calculate the Total Debt: Add up the amounts of all your liabilities to get the total debt.

Calculate Your Net Worth: To calculate your net worth, subtract your total debt from your total assets. The formula is:

Net Worth = Total Assets - Total Debt

The importance of this practice is to consider how keeping track of your net worth regularly can be a difference-maker for your financial well-being. Just as updating your assets and liabilities during changes helps you maintain accuracy, seeking clarity in life and business can offer insights that lead to better decisions.

Expanding on the benefits of understanding your net worth, setting financial goals to increase it over time is like setting a course for success. Similar to focusing on reducing debts and growing assets, directing your efforts toward strategic goals in life and business can steer you towards sustainable growth. Just as your net worth might experience fluctuations, your progress may have ups and downs, but the overall trend should be upward. Monitoring your financial health ensures you stay aligned with your objectives and adapt to changes effectively.

Let's delve into the distinction between "working in a business" and "working on a business." Validating this concept, think of "working in a business" as the hands-on engagement that keeps things running smoothly. Much like being directly involved in day-to-day operations, understanding immediate challenges and addressing them is vital.

Expanding on the benefits of comprehending the difference, "working on a business" shifts your focus from the immediate to the visionary. Just as setting goals and creating systems helps ensure the future success of your business, seeking a strategic perspective in life can lead to innovation and long-term sustainability. In essence, both aspects are like complementary gears in a well-oiled machine. Just as managing the present and shaping the future are essential for business growth, aligning your short-term tasks with your long-term goals in life can lead to a balanced and fulfilling journey.

For example, let's say you're a sales representative in a bakery. The "in the business" side involves selling pastries to customers, while the "working on the business" aspect could mean suggesting new products, exploring marketing strategies, and analyzing market trends. Similarly, grasping the difference between immediate tasks and visionary planning ensures your business navigates changes with agility and stays on course for long-term success.

Frequently, I engage in conversations with people, asking them a seemingly simple question: "What is your business?" It's intriguing how often the response revolves around their active profession, such as being a banker, lawyer, or doctor. Yet, I dig a bit deeper, posing another question: "Which bank do you own?" Often, the answer is a resounding "No, I work there." This illustrates a common confusion between the concepts of active and passive businesses, a distinction that holds profound significance.

Their active business involves their primary source of income, such as being a banker, but it's crucial to recognize the importance of having their own separate businesses. For instance, investing in stocks, real estate, or intellectual property implies ownership or partial ownership of a business. Herein lies an inherent truth: while school equips us with valuable knowledge and skills, it can inadvertently shape our identity in ways that limit our perspective. A focus on culinary studies might lead to becoming a chef, legal studies may result in becoming an attorney, and mastering auto mechanics could pave the way to becoming a mechanic.

However, the challenge arises when one becomes what they study, dedicating their efforts solely to their active business. A missed opportunity lies in neglecting the pursuit of robust passive business income. The consequence? A life spent predominantly working "in" business rather than "on" the business. The road to financial freedom and achieving your FUN Goal requires a shift in perspective and emphasis on nurturing and growing passive income streams from an early stage.

Consider this a call to action, urging individuals to allocate time, energy, and resources to cultivate their passive income avenues alongside their active professions. It's a journey toward balance, where both active and passive business endeavors coexist harmoniously. By embracing this mindset and actively nurturing passive income sources, you pave the way for financial autonomy and a future where you're not just working in your business but actively shaping and benefiting from it.

Dimes and Dreams

Investing when you're young is crucial. It's normal to feel overwhelmed when you realize you're responsible for planning and saving for your future. But don't worry—take it one step at a time. Remember the day you discovered what a "digital investment advisor" was? It felt like a weight lifted off your shoulders, giving you the confidence to take control of your finances.

These digital investment advisors make finance much less intimidating. No need to deal with the scary thought of talking to a bank salesperson. Trust me, that's a game-changer. It's as simple as saving a dime on a dollar. And here's the best part: they're not here to lecture you. You've teamed up with investors and financial experts who get you, making investing enjoyable and stress-free.

And you know what? The only thing you might regret is not starting sooner. Seriously, you'll look back and wish you had jumped in earlier. So why wait? Give it a shot. Your future self will thank you for taking that first step. Your future self will be high fiving your present self.

The Father and Son Lesson

Picture a father and his son sharing a special moment. The father hatches a unique plan to teach his son about the value of time and money. "Hey, Son," he begins, "I've got an interesting idea to share with you. You know how I work hard to earn money for the things we need and want?" The son nods, setting the stage for an enlightening journey.

The son's eyes widen in surprise. "A dime for every dollar you spend on what I want? That sounds like a lot!" The father smiles and says, "Exactly. It's a way to help you understand that every dollar represents time and effort. When we spend money, we're also spending the time we worked hard for." Curious, the son asks, "But why dimes?"

"Dimes are a little reminder of the value of time," the father explains. "Each dime you give me is like a small piece of your time. As you give those dimes, you'll start thinking about what's truly worth spending money on." Whenever the son asks for something, he contributes a dime for every dollar spent.

As the days turn into weeks, a change begins to take place. The son starts thinking more carefully about what he truly wants before asking his father. "Is this something I want, or is it something I really need?" he ponders. He becomes more thoughtful, weighing whether the item is worth giving up a piece of his time for. The father notices his son counting dimes before making a contribution, considering the value of his time and money.

One day, as they walk together, the son shares his realization. "You know, Dad, money isn't just about buying things. It's about how much time we spend working for it. I want to make sure I spend my time on things that really matter." The father's face beams with pride as he listens. "You've got it, Son! Money is a tool that empowers us to create memories, chase our dreams, and make a positive impact. By understanding the connection between time and money, you're already setting yourself up for a future filled with wise choices and meaningful experiences."

With the lesson of dimes and dreams, the son's outlook on money transforms. He begins evaluating the value of his time and the worth of the things he considers buying. The father and son share not just a lesson but a journey of understanding. They explore the world of money, time, and dreams together, ready to face challenges and seize opportunities side by side.

The Red Car Theory

Have you ever heard of the "Red Car Theory"? Imagine you're driving to work, and I ask you how many red cars you saw on the way. You might not have paid much attention, right? But what if, before you left your house, I told you I'd give you $100 for every red car you spotted during your commute? Suddenly, your perspective changes, and you start actively looking for red cars.

This concept applies not only to spotting red cars but also to life and business. Opportunity is all around us, just like those red cars. However, if you wake up every day and aren't actively looking for opportunities, you might miss them. They could be right in front of you, waiting at a red light, or parked at the coffee shop. They could be staring you in the face, but if you're not actively seeking them, you won't see them. So, keep your eyes open because opportunities are everywhere, waiting to be seized.

It's Okay to Be Used: Embracing Purpose in Your Journey of Becoming (YOUR JOB)

John had always been a dependable friend, the kind of person everyone turned to in times of need. Whether it was helping a neighbor move furniture, offering a listening ear to a colleague going through a tough time, or staying late at work to ensure a project met its deadline, John was always there. Over time, however, he began to feel worn out and unappreciated. One evening, after helping yet another friend solve a crisis, he sat down with his mentor, Sarah, and voiced his frustrations.

Sarah listened intently and then shared a perspective that changed John's outlook. "John," she said, "it's okay to be used, as long as you understand your purpose and ensure that your efforts are meaningful. Being of service to others is one of the most fulfilling aspects of life, but it's crucial to differentiate between being used and being useful."

To appreciate the concept of being used positively, we must first distinguish between being useful and being used uselessly. Being useful means contributing in ways that align with your purpose and values, creating value for others and yourself. Conversely, being used uselessly involves expending effort on tasks or relationships that do not bring fulfillment, growth, or a sense of accomplishment.

Recognizing and embracing your purpose is essential to ensure that being used leads to positive outcomes. When you understand your purpose, you can focus on activities that matter, contribute to your goals, and bring satisfaction. This purposeful use of your time and energy transforms the feeling of being used into a source of pride and joy.

The journey of becoming (JOB) is an ongoing process of growth, learning, and self-discovery. In both life and business, this journey involves understanding your strengths, recognizing opportunities to serve, and finding fulfillment in your contributions.

In life, being useful means leveraging your skills, time, and energy to support others while also nurturing your well-being. For example, volunteering at a local shelter, mentoring a young professional, or simply being a reliable friend or family member are ways to be useful. These acts of service not only benefit others but also enhance your sense of purpose and fulfillment.

In business, being useful translates to creating value for your organization, colleagues, and customers. This could mean leading a project that drives significant revenue, developing a new product that meets customer needs, or fostering a positive work environment. When your work aligns with your purpose, it becomes more than just a job; it becomes a meaningful part of your journey.

To embrace purpose practically, start by identifying your purpose. Reflect on your passions, skills, and the impact you want to make. Understanding your purpose helps you focus on being usefully used. Set boundaries to ensure that you do not deplete your energy on useless tasks. Learn to say no when necessary.

Regularly assess the value of your contributions. Are your actions aligned with your purpose? Are they making a positive impact? Look for ways to serve that resonate with your goals and values. Whether in your personal life or career, choose activities that bring satisfaction and growth.

Being useful should not come at the cost of your well-being. Ensure that you take care of yourself while helping others. Surround yourself with individuals who share your values and support your purpose. These relationships can provide encouragement, inspiration, and collaboration opportunities.

As we navigate our journey of becoming, the distinction between useful and useless becomes increasingly clear. By embracing purpose and focusing on usefulness, we can lead lives of significance and success. Whether in personal growth or business endeavors, the power of purpose ensures that every action we take is meaningful and impactful. Let usefulness be your guiding principle and watch as your journey transforms into a legacy of value and fulfillment.

Let's dive a bit more into "YOUR JOB," or as we like to put it, "Your Journey of Becoming." It's your personal adventure of transformation, growth, and evolution. It's all about embracing your uniqueness and becoming the person you've always aspired to be. This journey encompasses your pursuit of education, your quest for success, your emergence as a leader, and your voyage toward ultimate freedom. Here, you step into your own strength, unleash your potential, and embark on the incredible voyage of becoming the finest version of yourself.

A job isn't merely the tasks you perform; it's a reflection of the path you tread as you navigate through these distinct phases. Occasionally, we might find ourselves a bit stuck in our current circumstances. But instead of fixating on the present, our gaze should be on shaping our future.

The journey unfolds along four distinct lanes, each paving the way for your evolution:

- Employee: At the outset, we step into the world as employees, lending our time and expertise to established organizations. This phase is about learning the ropes, accumulating experience, and constructing the foundation for our professional voyage.

- Solo Entrepreneur: As we advance, the entrepreneurial spark ignites, urging us to venture forth independently. In this stage, we emerge as solo entrepreneurs, charting our own course and launching endeavors as freelancers or self-reliant consultants.
- Small Business Owner: Moving forward, we delve into the realm of small business ownership. This phase involves nurturing and cultivating a business that extends beyond individual efforts. As small business proprietors, we confront challenges head-on, fine-tune strategies, and broaden our horizons.
- CEO: Here, we ascend to the role of the Chief Executive Officer, the visionary leader of a thriving enterprise. In this stage, we steer larger organizations, shaping their trajectory, making pivotal decisions, and propelling growth.

Navigating Multiple Lanes

Guess what? You can navigate multiple lanes simultaneously. Let's use a teacher who wears different hats as an example:

By day, they embrace the role of an Employee, contributing their teaching skills and expertise within the school system.

In the evening, they shift into the lane of the Solo Entrepreneur, offering their specialized guidance as a tutor.

Additionally, they venture into the lane of a Small Business Owner by expanding their impact beyond individual tutoring sessions.

Mastering Your Craft
=====

As you begin your journey through the different stages of "YOUR JOB," one key principle stands out: the pursuit of mastery in your craft. This principle centers around the idea that to attain world-class expertise in any field, dedicating approximately 10,000 hours to deliberate practice is crucial. This breaks down to eight hours per day, five days a week, for fifty weeks a year. In essence, committing to this focused practice regimen can lead to mastery within just five years.

Embracing multiple lanes offers diversity, flexibility, and opportunities for growth. It allows individuals to leverage their skills, create multiple streams of income, and explore different facets of their industry. It's about embracing the dynamism of today's world and maximizing the potential of your journey.

Thriving, In the Black
=====

"Thriving, In the Black" places the spotlight squarely on YOU! Think of it as a treasure map guiding you toward personal growth, financial liberation, and boundless opportunities. Just as a CEO navigates a company, you hold the reins to steer your life toward triumph, contentment, and abundance. It's a journey unlike any other, an adventure brimming with excitement and promise.

Imagine you're in the driver's seat of a high-speed race car. Every turn you take, every decision you make, it's all under your control. The twists and turns in the journey of life are your challenges and opportunities, and you have the power to navigate them with finesse and precision.

But just like any CEO, you need a plan. And that's where "Thriving, In the Black" comes into play. This book is your ultimate guide to becoming the best CEO of your own life. It's like a treasure map that leads you through the exciting landscapes of personal growth, financial wisdom, and a deeper understanding of what truly matters.

Mastering Time Management

No complicated jargon here, just straightforward tips to help you get more done in your day.

First up, the early bird approach. If you're up for it, try waking up an hour earlier. Or, if you're more of a night owl, consider going to bed an hour later. But hey, life isn't always that simple, right? We all juggle different tasks, and sometimes, squeezing in an extra hour feels like solving a Rubik's cube. And here's the thing, whether you're rolling in riches or counting pennies, time is something you can't get back. It's like a limited-edition item, and you're the keeper. So, let's talk about a simple trick to help you take control of your time.

For the next couple of days, record how you spend your time. Break it down into 30-minute chunks. It might sound a tad meticulous, but here's the magic: when you start seeing where your time is going, it's like shining a spotlight on your choices. Suddenly, you're aware of how you're spending those precious moments. And guess what? Awareness leads to change. Once you notice those minutes slipping by, you'll naturally start making different choices. It's like having an accountability buddy, but it's you watching yourself. That TV show marathon might not seem so tempting when you realize you could be investing that time into something more meaningful.

Zoom out for a second and apply this to life and business. The lesson here is about intentionality. Just like you're managing your time, you can manage your life and career. Think of it as being the director of your own movie. You choose the scenes, the plot twists, and the main character: you.

When you master time management, you're not just getting things done; you're getting the right things done. You're carving out space for personal growth, meaningful experiences, and even those business breakthroughs you've been dreaming about. You're creating a life by design, not by default.

It's a ripple effect. When you're intentional with your time, you're showing up for yourself, your loved ones, and your goals. You're building a life that aligns with your values, and you're making a statement to the world that you're in charge.

So, start your 30-minute chronicles, become the time boss you were meant to be, and watch the dominoes of efficiency, success, and fulfillment fall into place. Your journey to a more productive and purposeful life begins with these simple choices. And remember, each tick of the clock is a chance to make a difference. Your time is now.

Teamwork!

It's perfectly fine to seek assistance; there's no shame in it. Just like a soldier facing a barrier, you have a mission to fulfill. If you find yourself wounded and in need of a helping hand to lift you up, remember the wisdom of Marcus Aurelius: if you're hurting and not seeking help, you can't be the best version of yourself, whether as a person, a professional, a partner, or a parent. None of us exist in isolation; we all rely on others. It's important to admit mistakes and reach out for support when needed. Asking for help doesn't make you weak; it makes you stronger and better equipped to face life's challenges.

Let me tell you a story. Once upon a time, a man found himself lost while driving through the countryside. As he attempted to consult a map, he accidentally swerved off the road and ended up stuck in a ditch. Although he emerged unscathed, his vehicle was deeply mired in mud. Realizing he couldn't free himself alone, he decided to seek assistance from a nearby farm.

Approaching the farmer, he asked for help in getting his car out of the ditch. The farmer pointed to an old, decrepit mule standing in a field and confidently said, "Warwick can get you out of that ditch." The man hesitated, looking at the mule and then at the farmer, who merely repeated, "Yep, old Warwick can do the job." Curiosity piqued, the man thought he had nothing to lose and agreed to the plan. The two men and the mule made their way back to the ditch. The farmer harnessed the mule to the car, and with a snap of the reins, he shouted, "Pull, Fred! Pull, Jack! Pull, Ted! Pull, Warwick!" The mule started pulling, and astonishingly, the car was pulled right out of the ditch.

Amazed and grateful, the man thanked the farmer, patted the mule named Warwick, and couldn't resist asking, "Why did you call out all of those names before you called Warwick?" With a grin, the farmer explained, "Old Warwick is blind. As long as Warwick believes he's part of a team, he doesn't mind pulling. It's all about that encouragement and sense of care. If you truly believe you can do it, you'll witness some incredible results."

Teamwork is like that magic ingredient that makes things happen. When Warwick, the mule, felt he was part of a team, he gave his all without hesitation. The same principle applies to us. When we feel that sense of unity and purpose, we're more motivated to put in our best efforts.

Think about it: when you know your teammates have your back and you're all working toward a common goal, it creates a powerful synergy. The encouragement and care you receive, and give in return, become the driving force behind your actions.

Just like Warwick's belief in being part of a team mattered, your belief in your team and yourself can lead to extraordinary outcomes. It's that shared sense of purpose and confidence that paves the way for remarkable results.

Let's dive into the concept of building your ultimate support team to navigate tough times and transform challenges into opportunities. Think of this team as your go-to crew, there to guide you through the journey. There are five key roles, or "JOBs," that you should consider having on your team: the mentor, teacher, guide, instructor, and coach. These roles are like different puzzle pieces that fit together to form a complete picture of support and growth in various aspects of your life.

First, there's the mentor. Imagine having that wise friend who's been through it all and is ready to share their experiences. A mentor provides guidance based on their own life journey, helping you navigate challenges with the benefit of their wisdom.

Next up is the teacher. Think of this role as your knowledgeable friend who loves explaining things. Teachers are there to help you learn new skills and gain valuable knowledge, whether in a classroom setting or in everyday life.

Guides are your short-term advisors, assisting you in specific situations or tasks. They offer expert insights to help you tackle challenges and make informed decisions.

An instructor teaches you specific techniques or skills in a particular area. Their expertise helps you acquire practical abilities that are directly applicable to your goals.

Last but not least, your coach is like your motivating partner who helps you excel in your chosen pursuits. They focus on your strengths, set achievable goals, and provide guidance to help you reach your full potential.

To sum it up:

- Mentors share experiences and advice.
- Teachers explain things and impart knowledge.
- Guides help you with specific tasks.
- Instructors teach particular skills.
- Coaches boost you to reach your goals.

Just like a successful sports team needs players with different positions and skills, you need these five roles in your support crew to ensure you're equipped to handle whatever comes your way. Building your team with the mentor, teacher, guide, instructor, and coach gives you a well-rounded set of perspectives and expertise to conquer challenges and seize opportunities in every area of your life. See, being part of a team involves understanding these roles and how they contribute to your long-term success. With teamwork, guidance, and the right mindset, you can achieve incredible results, just like Warwick did when he believed in his team.

The Fragile Thread of Trust

Trust, like a delicate thread, weaves the intricate fabric of our relationships, whether in life, business, or even the realm of credit. It's the foundation upon which bridges of understanding are built, and it has the power to connect people, nations, and opportunities. Yet, trust is so fragile that when it shatters, the sound reverberates with the echo of betrayal.

In life, consider the relationships that enrich our lives: friendships, families, partnerships. Trust is the glue that binds these connections. It's the unwavering belief that the ones we hold dear will be there, not just in times of joy, but also in moments of challenge. When trust exists, doors to shared dreams swing wide open, and the world becomes a canvas for shared experiences. This is when you're in the black in these relationships.

When trust falters, however, cracks form in the foundation of relationships. The fabric of understanding tears, and betrayal becomes a bitter note in what was once a harmonious symphony. Broken promises, hidden truths, and shattered confidence can taint even the most profound bonds. The challenge then becomes the painstaking process of rebuilding, of stitching back together the thread of trust that once held everything in place.

In the realm of business, trust forms the cornerstone of every transaction. Suppliers, clients, partners, they all depend on the assurance that their interests will be honored. When trust prevails, deals flourish, collaborations thrive, and prosperity follows. Just as nations engage in treaties built on trust, businesses engage in contracts founded on the belief that promises will be fulfilled.

Yet, as in life, the fragility of trust in business is ever-present. A single breach of trust can lead to a cascade of repercussions. A missed deadline, a broken agreement, a lack of transparency, these can unravel a carefully woven tapestry of partnerships. Leaving you in the red. The trust deficit created by such instances often takes time and effort to mend. And while bridges can be rebuilt, the echoes of betrayal linger in the minds of those who experienced it.

Enter the world of credit scores, where trust takes on a numerical form. It's a measure of financial reliability, a mirror reflecting our history of debt and repayment. Just as nations are rated by their financial credibility, individuals are evaluated by their creditworthiness. A good credit score opens doors to favorable interest rates, while a poor one can shut them, limiting opportunities for financial growth.

Building and maintaining trust in credit is essential. Borrowers must demonstrate their commitment to honoring their financial obligations. Conversely, lenders must maintain transparency and provide reliable terms. It's a delicate balance, and when trust is maintained, individuals gain access to opportunities for better living and financial security.

However, if trust in credit crumbles, its effects are far-reaching. A history of unpaid debts and defaulted loans can cast long shadows on one's credit score. The echoes of these missteps can hinder future financial endeavors, limiting access to loans, mortgages, and even rental agreements.

In life, business, and credit, trust is the cornerstone of relationships, transactions, and opportunities. It's a fragile thread that weaves our world together, capable of withstanding adversity but equally prone to unraveling when not treated with care. The lesson here is that trust must be nurtured, respected, and protected. For in the absence of trust, bridges collapse, foundations crack, and the echoes of betrayal remain a haunting reminder of what was lost.

The Power of Good Credit

You might not believe it, but having good credit is like having a superpower that can help you build wealth. And I'm here to show you how this works without getting into all the complicated stuff.

Let's start with the basics. Good credit isn't just about borrowing money. It's like having a secret key that unlocks doors to better deals. When you've got good credit, banks and lenders trust you more, and they give you loans and credit cards with lower interest rates. That means you get to keep more of your money instead of paying it to the bank. Pretty neat, huh?

Now, picture this: you're planting seeds of investments, and they're growing into towering trees of success. With good credit, you can borrow money for investments at lower interest rates. This means your investments have a chance to grow faster. And guess what? If you make clever investment choices, your net worth could double down the road.

But hold on, it's not just about cash. Having good credit is like holding a golden ticket to cool experiences. People trust you more, whether in business or personal life. Your reputation shines as bright as your credit score. With good credit, you might score a lower interest rate, which could cut your monthly payments in half. That's more cash in your pocket every single month. And here's the juicy part! As you keep paying and your home's value goes up, your net worth could skyrocket too.

Now, it's not just about dollars; it's about life lessons. Good credit and smart choices can swing open doors of opportunity for you. Whether you're eyeing a new home, kicking off a business, or just embracing life, good credit gives you that head start you've been looking for.

Take care of your credit score, make savvy financial moves, and watch the rewards roll in. It's like cultivating a garden of financial wins, and with good credit, your dreams could blossom into reality. Your future self will give you a high-five for paving the way to a brighter and richer tomorrow. Get ready to crank up your FUN Score and unlock those goals faster!

Entering the Red

In the early stages of life, the weight of credit and debt might not be fully comprehended. The chains of debt, seemingly inconspicuous, wrap around us lightly, their presence almost imperceptible. It's only as time passes that we begin to sense their weight, gradually realizing that these chains have intertwined themselves in our financial narrative. Like threads that become too tight to ignore, these debts can accumulate quietly until the day comes when we must summon the courage to break free of them. The lesson lies in acknowledging the potential burden early on and understanding these chains of debt. Though initially unnoticeable, these chains can exert a profound influence on our financial well-being.

> *"Be careful, the chains of debt are often too light to be felt until they are too heavy to be broken."*
>
> -Dr. Robert S. Dayse

In the modern world, credit plays a significant role in shaping our financial landscape. It's not just about having a plastic card in your wallet; it's about understanding how credit can either set you up for success or pave the way for challenges. Let's dive into the importance of credit, decipher the varying levels of credit health, and unravel its impact on your FUN Score and journey towards your FUN Goal. Let's dive right in and decode the importance of credit in your journey towards financial freedom.

The Credit Spectrum is often divided into four major categories: excellent, good, fair, and poor. An excellent credit score typically ranges from 800 to 850, signaling impeccable financial behavior. Excellent credit is like having VIP access to the best deals and opportunities. With this badge of honor, lenders practically roll out the red carpet for you. Interest rates? They're as low as a limbo champion. Good credit (670-799) reflects responsible money management. Good credit? You're still in the game, though the perks might not be as extravagant. Fair credit (580-669) suggests some room for improvement. You're not in the danger zone, but things could be better. Poor credit (below 580) indicates significant credit challenges that need attention. It's a red flag that might raise eyebrows.

How does credit subtract or propel you towards your FUN Goal? Think of credit as either a tailwind pushing you forward or a headwind slowing you down. With excellent or good credit, you ride that tailwind, accelerating towards your financial milestones. Fair credit is like a mild headwind; it adds a bit of resistance but doesn't stop you. On the other hand, poor credit could be like a strong headwind, making your journey more challenging.

Let's talk about credit. It can be a friend or a foe on your path to your FUN Goal. Affecting your FUN Score, which stands for Financially Unrestricted Number, credit acts like a mirror showing your financial freedom potential. Top-notch credit can give your FUN Score a boost, unlocking more financial opportunities. Good credit keeps your score healthy, while fair credit might cause a slight dip. Unfortunately, poor credit can take a toll on your FUN Score, putting limits on your financial options.

Credit has a two-sided role when it comes to your FUN Goal. On one side, maintaining good or excellent credit helps drive you towards your FUN Goal. It does this by giving you access to better investments and financial tools. On the flip side, poor credit takes away from your progress. High interest rates on loans and credit cards can nibble at your potential passive income, slowing down your journey to financial freedom.

The Bottom Line is understanding the importance of credit isn't just about numbers; it's about leveraging opportunities and avoiding unnecessary obstacles. Keeping your credit in good shape can give you the financial flexibility and freedom you need to achieve your FUN Goal. Just as you invest in your education and business ventures, invest in understanding and managing your credit. A high FUN Score doesn't just happen; it's your passport to unlocking your financial dreams. So, as you move forward, remember that credit isn't just about numbers; it's about shaping your financial path and getting closer to living life on your terms.

Go to Work

Have you heard this? In the world of wrestling, who tends to come out on top more often, Russians or American wrestlers? The odds seem to favor the Russians most of the time. While American wrestlers who achieve victory are often celebrated as prodigies, the truth is rooted in their technical mastery. On the flip side, the Russian champions who proudly claim those gold medals often remain somewhat hidden from the spotlight. They're like the Michael Jordans of wrestling, but here's the twist: there's an abundance of them.

Let's uncover the secret behind their success. Russian wrestlers invest substantial time and effort into consistent, lengthy practice sessions while training. They're on a mission to sharpen their skills. In contrast, the American approach often revolves around intense training sessions on specific days like Monday, Wednesday, and Friday, with more relaxed days in between. But hold on, the Eastern Bloc has a unique strategy. Their focus is on volume loads of practice especially as they gear up for significant competitions. They go for short yet intense bursts, right when it matters the most.

Picture this scenario. There are two teams, Team A and Team B. You're part of Team A, while I'm on Team B. We both start with similar efforts and at the same pace. You dedicate yourself to hard work, training, or studying three times a week. Meanwhile, I'm putting in the work every single day. On average, I dedicate about 2 hours each day to self-improvement, just like you. But here's the twist, by the end of the year, I've managed to squeeze in 2 more practices per week compared to you. Over the entire year, I've amassed an extra 100 practice sessions compared to your count. And guess what? This gives me a substantial advantage.

The lesson here is the undeniable influence of consistency and volume. Although we might start off at the same place, it's the unwavering commitment to improvement that truly sets the stage for success. So, the next time someone wonders how someone may have gotten where they are you'll most likely have the answer. It all boils down to their relentless workday in and day out. That's precisely how you secure the winning position in the end.

Let's break down some straightforward guidelines for achieving success, both in business and personal growth. Here are three essential rules to keep in mind:

- Rule #1, Embrace Hard Work: First and foremost, recognize that there's no shortcut to success. Some might suggest that being clever means you don't have to put in the effort. However, that's not the right approach. Whether you're smart or not, the key is a strong work ethic. Have a clear mindset that you're prepared to put in the hard work required to reach your goals. Success doesn't come by chance; it comes from dedication and consistent effort.
- Rule #2, Mindful Money Management: Your financial decisions play a critical role in your journey to success. Especially when you're starting without significant capital, every dollar you earn should be strategically utilized. Put your earnings back into your endeavors and see them multiply. Over time, this approach builds your capital base. Managing expenses is equally crucial. Be vigilant about how

you spend and develop the skill of controlling your financial outflows.
- Rule #3, Focus on Your Niche: In any industry, specialization is key. Instead of spreading yourself thin by diversifying too quickly, channel your efforts into mastering one area. Concentrate on something you understand and are passionate about. As you gain expertise and proficiency, you can contemplate diversification down the line. Remember, success is often built on a foundation of in-depth knowledge and excellence in a specific domain.

These simple yet powerful rules set the groundwork for a prosperous future. Whether it's in business ventures or personal growth, keeping these principles at heart can pave the way for meaningful achievements over time.

Balance, Integration, or Harmony

In a landscape where personal and professional growth takes center stage, envision embarking on a journey towards a well-rounded life that encompasses both your personal passions and your career aspirations. Let's create a path that leads to growth, with practical examples that highlight the ultimate goal of achieving your FUN score and making your FUN Goal a reality.

First, let's explore the concept of work-life balance. It's all about managing your time effectively, ensuring that you allocate the right number of hours to both work and personal activities. Think of it as a scale, where you strive to maintain equilibrium. For instance, you might dedicate a specific number of hours to your job and the same amount to your hobbies or family time. This approach emphasizes dividing your day into distinct work and personal segments, allowing you to give equal attention to both realms.

On the flip side, work-life integration takes a different approach. Instead of strict boundaries, this concept focuses on blending your work and personal activities in a way that complements your lifestyle. It's about finding opportunities to weave work tasks into your personal time and vice versa. For example, you might respond to work emails while waiting for your kid's soccer practice to finish. This approach encourages flexibility and seeks to eliminate the rigid separation between work and your personal life.

Let's introduce work-life harmony, a concept that adds a deeper layer of meaning to your journey. It's not just about how you use your time or what tasks you accomplish; it's about why you invest your time in certain activities. Work-life harmony is achieved when you align your actions with your core values and motivations. This means that the activities you engage in, both at work and in your personal life, resonate with your sense of purpose. It's about feeling fulfilled because your efforts align with your inner aspirations.

To truly achieve work-life harmony, consider viewing yourself as a whole person with interconnected roles. Imagine your career, your family life, your hobbies, and your personal growth all fitting together like pieces of a puzzle. When you pursue your passions and fulfill your responsibilities in a way that makes sense to you, that's when you've struck the perfect chord of harmony.

For instance, let's say you're passionate about environmental sustainability. You might integrate your passion into your career by seeking out opportunities for eco-friendly initiatives within your company. In your personal life, you could engage in volunteer work that aligns with your values. As a result, your actions at work and in your personal endeavors resonate with a common purpose, achieving harmony.

In this journey towards personal and professional growth, your FUN score and FUN Goal become the guiding stars. Your FUN score reflects how well you're aligning your actions with your values and aspirations. It's a measure of how much fulfillment, uniqueness, and newness you're experiencing in your life. As you progress on this path, you'll find that integrating your work and personal passions, along with harmonizing your actions with your core values, leads to a higher FUN score.

Ultimately, the most beneficial personal growth and professional success emerge when you're not just going through the motions but creating a symphony of purpose and meaning in everything you do. Your journey towards a balanced, integrated, and harmonious life is a testament to the fact that it's not about striving for perfection but about weaving a tapestry of experiences that reflect who you are and where you are going.

CHAPTER FOUR

Starting the Business of YOU

The familiar phrase "Ready, Set, Go" takes on a whole new meaning when it comes to embarking on the journey of building "YOU." And here's the exciting twist: YOU already exist! It's not about creating a new version of yourself; it's about discovering and nurturing the incredible potential that's already within.

Let's break it down:

Ready: It all starts with your mindset, attitude, and perspective. Are you in the right headspace to embrace this journey of self-discovery and growth? Being ready means being open to change, eager to learn, and willing to step outside your comfort zone. It's about giving yourself permission to explore the depths of your capabilities.

Set: Think of this as the phase where you're setting the stage for success. You're not just jumping in blindly; you're crafting a plan, setting measurable goals, and defining the path you want to follow. It's like plotting your course on a treasure map, marking the spots where you'll uncover the hidden gems within yourself.

Go: Now it's time to take action! You've prepared yourself mentally, you've charted your course, and now it's all about putting one foot in front of the other. The journey of building "YOU" is an active one. It's about engaging with life, seizing opportunities, and making strides towards your goals. It's like embarking on a thrilling adventure where the real treasures lie within.

Speaking of treasures, let's delve into the four dimensions of "inter-prizes" that make up the universe within you. Imagine yourself as the boss of a bustling city, where each cell plays a unique role to keep the whole operation running smoothly. It's like being in charge of an intricate orchestra, where every instrument contributes to creating beautiful music.

As you venture into the journey of building "YOU," remember that the treasures within are waiting to be discovered. It's a journey of readiness, preparation, and action, all guided by your desire to uncover the remarkable potential that's been there all along. Your universe within is a realm of endless possibilities, and the adventure is just beginning!

Let's meet some of the superstars of this incredible show. You've got the cell leaders, who are like the cool bosses of organs such as your heart, brain, liver, and more. They make sure everything runs like clockwork, just like a conductor leading a mesmerizing orchestra. Then there are the patrol cells, these are like vigilant superheroes patrolling your blood vessels to keep the peace and order intact.

Imagine you get a little scratch—no problem, because your very own superhero repair squad leaps into action. First, the blood-clotting team jumps in to stop the bleeding. Then, the tissue and skin teams work their magic to mend and seal the area. It's almost like having an exclusive team of experts dedicated to fixing you up!

Think about a sneaky intruder trying to cause chaos in your body, like a pesky bacterial infection. Well, no worries, because your memory cells are right on it! They snap a picture of the intruder and check their records for any past run-ins. If they've dealt with this troublemaker before, they summon the right attack team to neutralize the threat. If it's a newcomer, they create a new strategy and call in all the attack teams to save the day. Talk about being prepared!

But hold on, the surprises don't end there! Your body has its very own pharmacy, brewing up any healing potion you might need. It's as if you have a secret superhero lab creating just the right remedy. So, what's the ultimate goal of the 100 trillion cells in your body? It's simple: to keep you alive and well, working tirelessly every single moment, 24/7!

You Are the Commander-in-Chief

And here's the coolest twist: YOU are the head honcho, the commander-in-chief! Your thoughts, your feelings, and your beliefs are the guiding force for your cells. They're like your devoted army, ready to follow your lead without hesitation. If you believe you'll catch a cold, they're on it. But here's the exciting part: you have the power to turn things around for the better!

Don't forget, your cells listen closely to every thought and every feeling you have. So, let's shower them with positive vibes and healthy beliefs. Believe in your strength, envision yourself in great health, and watch your cells work their incredible magic. It's like having a league of allies dedicated to your well-being! Take the reins of your body's remarkable enterprise and witness how your reactions and beliefs can shape your health and your life. Your body is a superhero's paradise, and YOU have the power to make it flourish!

Emotions vs. Feelings: The Deeper Layer

Let's explore the intriguing world of emotions versus feelings for a moment. There's a tendency to regard our feelings as the ultimate truth, but here's the inside scoop: feelings are more like reactions. Think of them as the alarm bells that ring when something seems a little off.

Imagine this, feelings are like responses to wounds we might not even be aware of. It's like having a minor scratch that we never really tended to properly. Over time, that scratch might start bothering us, even if we can't see it. And our feelings? Well, they're a bit like that too—they're signals indicating that something requires our attention.

Navigating feelings can be tricky. They're not the entire story, and they don't always provide the full picture. It's as if our body is saying, "Hey, slow down! There's something beneath the surface that needs healing." But here's the twist: feelings aren't set in stone. They can shift and transform as we learn and grow. So, the next time you find yourself caught up in a particular feeling, take a moment to ask, "What's really happening here? Is there a deeper layer I should be exploring?"

This is all part of the voyage to truly understanding ourselves and delving into the depths of our inner world. While feelings might resemble surface ripples, it's in the ocean beneath that the real currents flow.

As we dive deeper into these inner realms, let's explore the second dimension of the emotional body, or as we fondly refer to it, The Heart's Symphony. Imagine this dimension as a magnificent orchestra, conducting a symphony of our emotional experiences. Here, the nervous system dances to the melodies of emotions, hormones play their tunes, and the sense of touch and the rhythm of tears each play their distinct part.

The emotional body isn't only about experiencing emotional highs and lows; it's also a repository for our past emotional encounters. Visualize it as a storage room filled with memories interwoven with emotions like anger, sadness, jealousy, fear, guilt, resentment, and shame. These emotions settle into the depths of our subconscious and unconscious minds, forming emotional blocks that can hinder our growth.

In this emotional realm, deep wounds find their dwelling place. If we haven't acknowledged and healed these wounds, the negative vibes they emit can cast shadows over our lives, weighing us down and anchoring us to our emotions.

Here's where the connection to a large organization or enterprise comes into play. Just as a thriving organization requires a clear flow of communication and collaboration among its members, so does our emotional body. The energy flow from the mental realm to the emotional realm is like the communication network within a well-functioning enterprise. However, emotional wounds can act as roadblocks, causing disruptions in this flow much like bottlenecks in an organization's processes.

These emotional bottlenecks can lead to feelings of anxiety, stress, and heightened anger, affecting not only our emotional well-being but also impacting our physical health. Have you ever noticed yourself reacting in an unusual manner, in a way that doesn't quite align with your usual self? Those reactions might very well be linked to these hidden emotional blocks. Life often stages situations and encounters that unveil our emotional wounds, presenting us with the chance to confront and heal them.

Within this emotional theater, we also discover the treasures of positive feelings such as abundance, love, freedom, and joy. As we heal old wounds, these positive emotions come to the forefront. It's like unwrapping a gift of happiness and love that was present all along. And guess what? Just as within an enterprise, where the harmony between various teams leads to successful outcomes, the fusion of body language and emotions becomes a dynamic duo within us like personal interpreters unraveling the secret of our own functioning.

The Mental Body

The third dimension, the MENTAL BODY, is where your thoughts, attitudes, and the clarity of your mind come into play. Just as in a large organization or enterprise, where effective communication and clear strategies are crucial for success, your mental realm determines how smoothly your overall system functions. When things aren't aligned here, you might experience brain fog, a lack of creativity, or simply a feeling of being in a funk—similar to how inefficiencies in an organization can lead to a decline in performance.

Think of the mental realm as a vast theater, with starring roles for your thoughts, beliefs, desires, values, goals, and opinions. It's like the stage where you process information, learn, and decide where to focus your attention—much like the core decisions and strategies that an organization's leadership must make. Within this mental landscape, there are two primary actors: your egoic mind and your divine mind.

Imagine the egoic mind as a tool that you can use to shape your reality. It's all about setting intentions, making plans, and actively pursuing your goals—just like the way an organization's management sets targets and formulates plans for growth. Ideally, you'd activate your egoic mind when necessary and then allow it to rest, embracing the serenity of the divine mind—much like how successful organizations find a balance between planning and maintaining a mindful approach.

However, in many cases, just as organizations might become overly focused on day-to-day operations, most of us have lost touch with the concept of switching off our egoic mind. It often seems to be in a perpetual state of motion, like an engine that never ceases to generate thoughts.

When your mental realm is clear and calm, just as when an organization's leadership is aligned and focused, you're in a state of pure presence and harmony with your divine mind. It's akin to plugging into an abundant energy source. The mental body becomes a conduit, absorbing energy from the spiritual realm and channeling it before a single thought even takes shape—much like the way a well-organized and focused organization can implement strategies smoothly and efficiently.

However, when the egoic mind takes the reins—overthinking, overplanning, ruminating on the past, or adamantly clinging to opinions—that's when mental roadblocks emerge. Like how an organization might encounter obstacles in its decision-making process, these mental roadblocks hinder your clarity and creativity. They're like encountering detours on the path to mental effectiveness.

This third dimension, the mental body, is all about striking a balance. It's about finding that sweet spot between tapping into the potential of the egoic mind—just as organizations harness their strategies—and embracing the serene wisdom of the divine mind—mirroring the equilibrium between detailed planning and mindfulness in a successful enterprise. It's a journey where the key lies in navigating between these two dimensions, ultimately unlocking your mental prowess and clarity, much like a well-managed organization achieves its objectives through strategic planning and a mindful approach.

The Spiritual Body

The fourth dimension we're about to explore is the SPIRITUAL BODY, akin to the broader structure of a large organization or enterprise within the human body. Just as in a complex organization where different departments contribute to the overall success, the spiritual body represents your connection to something grander, something beyond the everyday realm.

Whether you call it the Universe, God, Source, Higher Self, Love, Life, or any other term—doesn't truly matter. What holds significance is the essence of this connection. It's about tapping into guidance and surrendering to a force larger than ourselves—similar to how a successful organization draws upon a shared vision and values to guide its operations.

You might be wondering whether this realm delves into religion or cultural beliefs. But it's more profound than that. It's about realizing our inherent oneness, understanding that we're all interconnected at a fundamental level—much like how a cohesive organization operates as a unified entity. This is where our true essence resides, much like the core values that underpin a well-established organization.

Within our spiritual body lies energy, akin to the vital energies that sustain a thriving organization. This energy flows into our mental self, much like how a company's strategies and vision flow into the decisions made by its leadership. When we're attuned to our spirituality, in a state of balance with this dimension, a sense of tranquility envelops us. Just as a well-organized organization operates calmly, we find the strength to confront our fears. We become aware of love's pervasive presence, much like the sense of camaraderie within a tightly knit team, and we place our trust in a higher power, like trusting the overarching goals of an organization's leadership. In this aligned state, we can manifest our aspirations with effortless efficiency, similar to how a successful organization brings its objectives to fruition.

Now, here's the captivating part: your spiritual self is inherently whole, untouched by wounds or hurts—resembling the enduring spirit of an organization. It's the alignment that might sometimes be off, akin to how an organization's practices might deviate from its core values. When we disconnect from our spiritual essence, it can create mental blocks, much like how misalignment within an organization can hinder progress. These blocks obstruct the flow of energy from the spiritual dimension to the mental realm, mirroring how dissonance between vision and execution can disrupt an organization's performance. It's like a dance of energies, and just as a well-orchestrated performance leads to success, finding harmony within the spiritual realm enhances our connection to our full potential—similar to how alignment with an organization's core values leads to its optimal functioning.

The Science of Financial Learning

Before we get into the basics of budgeting, investing, and all those practical money matters, it's crucial to understand how your brain plays a role in absorbing and retaining financial knowledge. After all, knowledge that doesn't stick is about as useful as a leaky bucket.

First things first, let's talk about how your brain processes information. Your brain is a complex and marvelous organ, but it doesn't always work the way you want it to, especially when it comes to learning new things.

When you encounter a new piece of financial information, like the difference between a traditional IRA and a Roth IRA, your brain has to process it, make sense of it, and then store it for later use. This process uses different mental skills like paying attention, understanding, and remembering it. Attention is like the bouncer at the nightclub of your brain. It decides what information gets in and what gets turned away at the door. The more focused your attention is on a financial concept, the more likely it is to stick. That's why it's crucial to find ways to engage your brain when learning about finances.

Understanding the material is the next step. It's not just about memorizing terms and formulas. For example, it's not enough to know that compound interest exists; you need to understand how it works and why it matters for your financial future.

Once you've paid attention and comprehended the material, your brain needs to store it in memory. Think of your memory as a storage room filled with boxes of information. Some boxes are labeled "important," and others are labeled "not so important." The key is to make sure financial knowledge ends up in the "important" boxes.

Lastly, there's recall—the ability to retrieve the information from memory when you need it. It's like trying to find that one specific box in a cluttered storage room. The better organized your storage room (your memory) is, the easier it is to retrieve what you need.

Now that you have a basic understanding of how your brain works in the learning process, let's talk about techniques to make financial knowledge stick.

- Spaced Repetition: Instead of cramming all your financial learning into a single session, spread it out over time. Review and revisit key concepts regularly. This technique reinforces your memory.
- Active Engagement: Don't just passively consume financial information. Engage with it actively. Take notes, ask questions, and discuss concepts with others. The more you engage, the more likely you are to remember.
- Visualization: Use mental imagery to visualize financial concepts. For instance, imagine your financial goals as vividly as possible. Visualization helps your brain create strong memory connections.

- Teach Others: Teaching is one of the best ways to learn. When you explain financial concepts to someone else, you reinforce your understanding and memory.
- Create Memory Aids: Create memory aids like acronyms or catchy phrases to remember complex information. For instance, "PEMDAS" helps you remember the order of operations in mathematics.
- Self-Testing: Test yourself on what you've learned. Practice recalling financial concepts regularly. This strengthens your ability to retrieve information when you need it.

Remember, your brain is a muscle, and like any muscle, it can be trained and strengthened. The more you understand how your brain processes financial information and use these techniques, the better you'll become at making financial knowledge stick.

Navigating Life's Financial Challenges

Life has a way of throwing curveballs when you least expect them, often in the form of financial challenges. Whether it's an unexpected medical expense, a sudden job loss, or a major home repair, these events can feel like storms on your financial horizon. But fear not, we're here to help you navigate through them.

Life is unpredictable. One moment everything seems fine, and the next, you're dealing with an unexpected expense. It could be a medical emergency, a car breakdown, or even a leaky roof. These situations can be stressful, but they're a part of life, and it's essential to be prepared.

Think of your emergency fund as your financial safety net. It's there to catch you when you fall, ensuring that unexpected expenses don't completely derail your financial stability.

- Start small: If you don't have an emergency fund yet, don't worry. Start small, even if it's just $500 or $1,000. Every little bit helps.
- Set a goal: Aim to save at least three to six months' worth of living expenses. This cushion can provide peace of mind during tough times.
- Automate savings: Set up automatic transfers to your emergency fund each time you get paid. This makes saving a consistent habit.
- Use windfalls: Consider directing unexpected windfalls, like tax refunds or work bonuses, into your emergency fund.
- Your savings: Keep your emergency fund in a separate savings account, away from your regular spending money, to reduce the temptation to dip into it for non-emergencies.

In addition to your emergency fund, contingency planning is another essential tool for navigating financial challenges. It involves thinking through various "what-if" scenarios and developing a plan for each.

- Job loss: What if you lose your job? How will you cover your living expenses while searching for a new one?
- Car breakdown: What if your car breaks down? Do you have a plan for alternative transportation?
- Medical expenses: What if you face unexpected medical expenses? Are you aware of your insurance coverage and options for managing bills?

Having contingency plans in place can help you respond more calmly and effectively when unexpected challenges arise.

Life's financial challenges can be daunting, but they don't have to derail your long-term financial goals. When a financial challenge arises, take a deep breath, and assess the situation. What exactly is the problem, and what are your options for addressing it?

- Prioritize essentials: Focus on covering essential expenses like housing, food, and utilities. Cut back on non-essential spending until the challenge is resolved.
- Seek resources: Explore resources that can help you during tough times. This might include unemployment benefits, community assistance programs, or negotiating with creditors.
- Use your emergency fund: If you have an emergency fund, now is the time to use it for its intended purpose. That's what it's there for, after all.
- Adjust goals: It's okay to temporarily pause or adjust some of your long-term financial goals while you navigate a challenge. Your financial journey is a marathon, not a sprint.
- Stay positive: Remember that financial setbacks are a part of life, and they don't define your overall financial health. Stay positive, be persistent, and keep working toward your goals.

Life's financial challenges can be tough, but they're not insurmountable. With careful planning, emergency funds, and a mindset of adaptability, you can weather these storms and stay on course toward your long-term financial objectives. In the next chapter, we'll explore another essential aspect of financial well-being: managing and ultimately overcoming debt.

Mastering the Mindset

When it comes to personal finance, it's not just about numbers and spreadsheets. Your mindset plays a significant role in your financial decisions and overall well-being. In this chapter, we're going to explore the psychology of money and techniques to help you develop a resilient and positive financial mindset.

Ever wondered why you make certain financial choices or why you feel a certain way about money? It's all about psychology. Your beliefs, attitudes, and emotions around money are deeply ingrained and can significantly impact your financial behaviors.

- Emotional impact: Emotions like fear, greed, and anxiety can drive impulsive financial decisions. For example, fear might make you sell your investments during a market downturn, potentially locking in losses.
- Cognitive biases: We all have cognitive biases that can lead to irrational financial decisions. Confirmation bias, for instance, can make you seek out information that confirms your existing beliefs while ignoring contradictory evidence.
- Societal influence: The spending habits of your peers and societal pressure can shape your own spending choices. The fear of missing out (FOMO) can lead to overspending to keep up with others.

Mindfulness Practices for Financial Well-being

Dating back to ancient Greece, the practice of using blinders on horses emerged in chariot racing. Their purpose was simple yet effective to maintain the horses' focus during the commotion of the race, preventing distraction from other horses, the crowd, or the surrounding environment.

Similarly, mindfulness acts as mental blinders in financial matters. Cultivating mindfulness enhances financial awareness and overall well-being, facilitating conscious financial decisions and clearer navigation of one's financial journey.

Here's how to apply mindfulness to your finances:

- Regular check-ins: Regularly take a few minutes to check in with your financial situation. Review your accounts, expenses, and progress toward your goals.
- Pause before purchasing: Before making a purchase, pause and ask yourself if it aligns with your values and goals. Avoid impulsive spending by taking a moment to reflect.
- Deep breathing: When facing financial decisions or stress, practice deep breathing exercises to calm your mind and reduce impulsive reactions.
- Gratitude journal: Keep a gratitude journal for your financial life, appreciating simple blessings like having a stable job or affording necessities.
- Visualization: Use visualization techniques to picture your financial goals, motivating you to stay on track towards success.

Developing a positive financial mindset and practicing mindfulness is an ongoing journey. Be patient with yourself and understand that setbacks are a part of the process. Over time, you'll become more resilient in the face of financial challenges and make more mindful and informed decisions. In the next chapter, we'll explore the importance of self-love and self-care in your financial journey.

Learning from Mistakes

Mistakes happen to the best of us, especially when it comes to personal finance. Maybe you made an ill-advised investment, overspent on a lavish vacation, or racked up credit card debt. Whatever the financial hiccup, the key is not to beat yourself up but to embrace the concept of financial resilience and learn from your mistakes. In this chapter, we'll delve into the power of bouncing back, featuring case studies of individuals who turned financial setbacks into success stories, and we'll provide strategies for recovering from financial mistakes and making lasting changes.

Financial resilience is the ability to adapt and recover from financial setbacks, no matter how big or small. It's about recognizing that everyone makes mistakes, and it's how you respond to those mistakes that matters most.

Acknowledge without judgment: The first step in resilience is acknowledging your financial missteps without judgment. Accept that you've made a mistake, and don't dwell on it.

- Learn from the experience: Treat every financial mistake as a learning opportunity. Ask yourself what led to the mistake and what you can do differently next time.
- Be flexible and adaptable: Be flexible and open to changing your financial habits and behaviors. Adaptation is key to overcoming challenges.
- Practice self-compassion: Be kind to yourself during financial setbacks. Self-blame and guilt can hinder your progress.

- Keep moving forward: Keep moving forward, even if progress is slow. Financial resilience is built over time through consistent effort.

To illustrate the power of financial resilience, let's look at a few case studies of individuals who faced significant financial setbacks and emerged stronger than ever.

Case Study 1: Emily's Debt Dilemma

Emily found herself drowning in credit card debt due to overspending and medical bills. Instead of spiraling into despair, she took action. She created a strict budget, negotiated lower interest rates on her credit cards, and started a side hustle. It took time, but Emily paid off her debt and built an emergency fund, proving that with determination and a plan, you can conquer financial setbacks.

Case Study 2: James's Investment Mishap

James invested a significant portion of his savings in a speculative stock that tanked. Instead of giving up on investing altogether, he educated himself, diversified his portfolio, and sought advice from a financial advisor. Over time, his investments grew, showing that even a big financial blunder can be a steppingstone to success.

Case Study 3: Mia's Career Crisis

Mia lost her job unexpectedly, sending her into a panic. Rather than settling for the first available job, she used the opportunity to reevaluate her career goals. She invested in retraining, expanded her network, and eventually landed a more fulfilling job with better pay. Mia's resilience led her to a brighter financial future.

So, what can you do when faced with financial mistakes?

- Assess the situation: Take a clear-eyed look at the extent of the mistake. Understand the financial impact and the root causes.
- Develop a plan: Develop a step-by-step plan for addressing the mistake. Whether it's paying off debt, rebuilding savings, or reevaluating your financial goals, having a plan is essential.
- Seek advice: Don't be afraid to seek advice from financial experts, mentors, or support groups. They can offer valuable insights and accountability.
- Monitor progress: Monitor your progress regularly. Celebrate small victories along the way, and adjust your plan as needed.
- Embrace resilience: Embrace the principles of financial resilience we discussed earlier. Accept, learn, adapt, show self-compassion, and persist.
- Set new goals: Use your mistakes as a springboard to set new, more achievable financial goals. This can reignite your motivation.

The road to financial success is rarely a straight line. It's okay to stumble along the way. What matters most is how you pick yourself up, learn from your mistakes, and continue moving forward. Financial resilience is not just about bouncing back; it's about bouncing forward, stronger and wiser.

Your Unique Financial DNA

In the world of personal finance, it's easy to get caught up in the pursuit of financial success defined by others. We often compare our financial situations to those of friends, family, or even celebrities, and in doing so, we lose sight of a fundamental truth: your financial journey is as unique as your fingerprint.

Just as Emily Nagoski's "Come As You Are" celebrates the individuality of our experiences and desires, this book on personal finance emphasizes that there is no one-size-fits-all approach to managing money. Your financial journey is personal, and it's time to embrace it as you are.

In the age of social media and instant access to the lives of others, it's all too easy to fall into the comparison trap. You see a friend's new car, a neighbor's home renovation, or a colleague's exotic vacation, and you may feel a sense of inadequacy or pressure to keep up.

The danger of these comparisons is that they can lead to financial decisions that aren't aligned with your values or goals. You might find yourself overspending to keep up appearances or investing in things that don't genuinely bring you happiness or security. The result? Financial stress and a sense of emptiness.

Just as your DNA determines your physical traits, your "Financial DNA" shapes your financial habits, values, and goals. It's a unique combination of your upbringing, experiences, beliefs, and aspirations. Understanding and embracing your Financial DNA is a crucial step in your financial journey.

- Family influence: Your family's financial history and values play a significant role in shaping your financial attitudes. Were your parents savers or spenders? Did they teach you about money management?
- Past experiences: Your past financial experiences, both positive and negative, influence your financial decisions. Have you experienced financial hardship or windfalls? How did those experiences impact your mindset?
- Beliefs about money: Your beliefs about money, success, and happiness are deeply ingrained. Do you believe that more

money equals more happiness? Do you view wealth as a measure of success?
- Financial goals: Your financial goals and aspirations are unique to you. What are your long-term financial dreams? What do you want to achieve with your money?

The key to a successful financial journey is to embrace your uniqueness. Your Financial DNA is a part of who you are, and it's neither good nor bad—it just is. It's the foundation upon which you can build a financial plan that aligns with your values and aspirations.

- Reflect on your financial background: Take time to reflect on your financial upbringing, experiences, beliefs, and goals. Understanding where you come from can shed light on your financial habits.
- Identify core values: Identify your core financial values. What truly matters to you? Is it financial security, freedom, generosity, or something else?
- Set personal goals: Your financial goals should be personal and meaningful to you. Whether it's buying a home, starting a family, traveling the world, or giving back, your goals should resonate with your values.
- Challenge societal norms: Question societal or peer pressures that don't align with your Financial DNA. Remember that what's right for someone else may not be right for you.
- Create a tailored plan: Build a financial plan that reflects your uniqueness. Your plan should help you achieve your goals while staying true to your values.

- Celebrate progress: Embrace each step of your financial journey, no matter how small. Celebrate your wins, and don't be too hard on yourself when things don't go as planned.

In a world that often prescribes cookie-cutter financial advice, remember that your Financial DNA sets you apart. It's the blueprint for your unique financial journey. By embracing it, you can build a financial future that reflects who you truly are and what you genuinely desire. In the chapters that follow, we'll explore how to create a financial plan that celebrates your uniqueness and helps you achieve your financial goals on your terms.

Customizing Your Financial Path

In the world of personal finance, there's no one-size-fits-all approach. Your financial journey is as unique as your fingerprint, and your path to financial mastery should reflect your values, aspirations, and circumstances. In this chapter, we'll explore the importance of customizing your financial path, tailoring financial goals to match your values, recognizing that your journey may differ from others, and creating a flexible financial plan that evolves with you.

The first step in customizing your financial path is aligning your financial goals with your values. Your values are the principles and beliefs that guide your life, and they should also guide your financial decisions.

Identify core values: Take time to identify your core values. What matters most to you in life? Is it family, adventure, freedom, or something else entirely?

Align goals with values: When setting financial goals, ensure that they align with your values. For example, if family is a core value, your financial goals might include saving for your children's education or planning family vacations.

- Prioritize goals: Rank your financial goals based on their alignment with your values. Prioritize those that are most meaningful to you.
- Review spending: Regularly review your spending to ensure it reflects your values and goals. Are you spending in ways that align with what you truly value?

It's essential to recognize that your financial journey may differ significantly from those of others, and that's perfectly okay. Society often places undue pressure on individuals to conform to certain financial norms or expectations. However, your financial path should reflect your individuality, not societal standards.

- Avoid comparisons: Refrain from comparing your financial situation to that of friends, family, or colleagues. Remember that everyone has different circumstances and goals.
- Reject timelines: Don't feel pressured to achieve certain financial milestones by a specific age. Your timeline should be based on your unique circumstances and aspirations.
- Celebrate uniqueness: Celebrate the aspects of your financial journey that make it unique. Embrace the choices and experiences that set you apart.
- Question societal expectations: Question societal expectations about money, success, and happiness. Are they aligned with your values and goals, or are they imposed by external pressures?

As you customize your financial path, it's essential to create a flexible financial plan that can adapt to your changing circumstances and evolving aspirations. Life is full of unexpected twists and turns, and your financial plan should be prepared to accommodate them.

- Set clear goals: Define your financial goals with specificity. The clearer your objectives, the easier it is to adapt your plan as needed.
- Include contingencies: Include contingencies in your plan for unforeseen expenses or changes in your financial situation. An emergency fund is an essential part of this.
- Review regularly: Periodically review your financial plan to ensure it remains aligned with your values and goals. Adjust as necessary to reflect changes in your life.
- Seek professional advice: Consider consulting with financial professionals who can help you create a flexible plan that accounts for various scenarios.
- Stay informed: Stay informed about changes in the financial landscape and how they might impact your plan. Being proactive can help you make timely adjustments.

Customizing your financial path isn't about rejecting financial norms or blindly following your desires; it's about aligning your financial journey with your values, recognizing your uniqueness, and creating a plan that allows for flexibility and adaptability. Your financial path should be a reflection of who you are, where you want to go, and how you want to live your life.

Overcoming Financial Barriers

In this chapter, we'll tackle the formidable challenge of overcoming financial barriers; those obstacles that can hinder your progress on the path to financial mastery. We'll explore how to identify and address these barriers, whether they involve debt, low income, or other financial challenges. We'll also discuss how to seek support and resources that align with your specific needs and, most importantly, how to find empowerment in taking control of your financial situation.

Before you can overcome financial barriers, it's crucial to identify them. These barriers can take many forms, and they often vary from person to person.

1. Debt: Debt can be a significant barrier to financial progress, particularly when it comes with high-interest rates.
2. Limited income: A limited income can make it challenging to cover basic expenses, let alone save or invest for the future.
3. Lack of savings: Without an emergency fund or savings buffer, unexpected expenses can create financial stress.
4. Financial literacy: A lack of financial knowledge and literacy can lead to poor money management decisions.
5. Job instability: Job loss or being underemployed can create instability in your financial life.
6. Health issues: Health issues or unexpected medical bills can strain your finances.
7. Family responsibilities: Supporting family members financially can be a significant barrier to achieving your own financial goals.

Once you've identified your financial barriers, the next step is to address them. While it may not be easy, it is possible to overcome these obstacles with determination and a strategic approach.

1. Debt repayment: Develop a debt repayment plan that focuses on high-interest debts first. Consider debt consolidation or negotiating with creditors to lower interest rates.
2. Increase income: Explore ways to increase your income, such as seeking better job opportunities, pursuing additional education or training, or starting a side business.
3. Build an emergency fund: Prioritize building an emergency fund by setting aside a portion of your income regularly. Start with small, manageable amounts and gradually increase your savings.
4. Financial education: Invest in your financial education by reading books, attending workshops, or taking online courses. Seek guidance from financial professionals if needed.
5. Job search: Network, update your resume, and actively search for job opportunities. Consider gig work or freelancing to supplement your income.
6. Healthcare planning: Negotiate medical bills when possible and explore healthcare assistance programs. Prioritize health insurance to protect against future medical costs.
7. Family discussions: Have open and honest conversations with family members about your financial situation. Set boundaries and seek financial assistance or government programs if available.

You don't have to navigate these financial barriers alone. There are numerous resources and support systems available to help you overcome these challenges.

1. Community resources: Research local non-profit organizations, community groups, or charities that provide financial assistance or financial literacy programs.
2. Government assistance: Explore government assistance programs for housing, food, healthcare, or unemployment benefits.
3. Financial counseling: Consider seeking the guidance of a certified financial counselor who can help you develop a personalized financial plan.
4. Online communities: Join online forums or communities where individuals share their experiences and strategies for overcoming financial barriers.
5. Support network: Lean on friends and family for emotional support and encouragement. Sometimes, just talking about your challenges can provide relief.

Overcoming financial barriers is not only about resolving immediate challenges; it's also about finding empowerment in taking control of your financial situation. When you confront and conquer these obstacles, you gain a sense of control over your financial destiny.

1. Set small goals: Break down your financial goals into small, achievable steps. Celebrate each milestone as you progress.
2. Track achievements: Keep a record of your financial achievements, no matter how minor they may seem. It's a tangible reminder of your progress.
3. Stay persistent: Financial barriers may not disappear overnight. Stay persistent and adaptable in your approach.
4. Celebrate successes: Acknowledge your successes, no matter how small. Celebrate your resilience and determination.

5. Share your journey: Consider sharing your journey with others. Your experiences can inspire and motivate those facing similar challenges.

Overcoming financial barriers is a testament to your resilience and determination. Remember that you are not defined by your obstacles; you are defined by your ability to overcome them. By identifying and addressing financial barriers, seeking support and resources, and finding empowerment in taking control, you can break through these barriers and continue on your path to financial mastery.

Your FUN Score (FUNS): Financially Unrestricted Number Score

Once, a professor walked into a classroom carrying a glass jar along with rocks, pebbles, and sand. The students watched with curiosity as he began arranging the elements inside the jar. First, he carefully placed the rocks into the jar until they filled it to the brim. Turning to the students, he asked if the jar was full, and they all nodded in agreement. Then, he proceeded to insert the pebbles into the jar, allowing them to settle into the spaces between the rocks. With a gentle shake, the pebbles found their place in the gaps. Once again, the professor asked the students if the jar was full, and they responded affirmatively.

Finally, he poured the sand into the jar, and it seeped through the tiny spaces left by the rocks and pebbles. Now, the jar truly appeared to be full. The professor's demonstration provided a profound lesson in prioritizing life's elements. By associating rocks with family, pebbles with career goals, and sand with minor concerns like arguments and ego conflicts, he underscored the importance of identifying what truly matters.

Let's dive into an exciting concept that could be your ticket to financial freedom; your "FUN Score." Think of it as a key that has the potential to unlock a new realm of financial possibilities in your life. As you explore the pages of this book, your familiarity with the term "FUN Score" might grow to match that of your home address. This number holds the power to reshape your financial landscape and lead you toward greater freedom.

Picture your "FUN Score" as a compass guiding you on the journey to financial liberation. It's like a secret combination that opens doors to a reality where your dreams can finally take shape. This unique number represents the financial threshold that ushers you into a life where you can live on your own terms, free from the burdens of bills and financial constraints. Your "FUN Score" empowers you to set clear financial goals and work towards achieving them.

Think of it as your personal treasure map. Once you've cracked the code and know your FUN Score, you're on a journey to make money work for you. It's not just about accumulating wealth; it's about making smart investments, wise financial choices, and watching your money grow like a well-nurtured garden.

Your FUN Score isn't just a number; it's your gateway to a life where you can chase your passions, explore new horizons, and embrace opportunities without hesitation. It's the number that holds the key to your aspirations. Every step you take towards reaching your FUN Score brings you closer to turning those aspirations into reality.

The analogy extends to our financial journey and the pursuit of our FUN Score. Just as the jar represents life's limited space, our financial resources have their limits too. By placing the rocks representing essential priorities like family and financial security into the jar first, we ensure that the most important aspects of our lives take precedence. This insightful lesson encourages us to be mindful of not allowing the jar to fill up prematurely with sand, symbolic of trivial matters and unnecessary distractions. Through effective prioritization and efficient allocation of resources, we create a harmonious balance where both the pebbles, representing career aspirations and personal ambitions, and the sand coexist without overwhelming the jar.

In essence, the lesson revolves around recognizing our core priorities, formulating a strategic plan, and investing our efforts in what holds true significance. Just as the professor's demonstration highlighted, a well-rounded approach in both life and finances prevents us from expending time and energy on less vital elements. Instead, we make space for what truly matters, paving the way for substantial experiences and a journey towards fulfillment and financial liberation.

Imagine your "FUN Score" as a silent financial guide, working behind the scenes to empower you with the ability to navigate life's choices, make informed decisions, and savor the rewards of authentic financial freedom. Let your "FUN Score" shine as a guiding star, leading you toward a future where each day is a new chapter filled with excitement, and you are the author of your own success story.

The Four Stages of Business Success

Let's delve into the beliefs I hold about the four stages of business success in life's journey: Survival, Security, FUN Score (Freedom), and Wealth. Let's break down each stage and explore their significance.

First up, we've got Survival. Imagine that you're in the midst of hustling, working hard to keep up with your expenses, and ensuring those bills are paid on time. It's like being in a constant battle to make ends meet, living from one paycheck to the next. Picture yourself treading water in a vast ocean, exerting effort just to stay afloat. During this phase, you find yourself in a position where your income is the main pillar of support. Any disruption, like missing a paycheck, could easily tip the balance and create financial instability. This Survival stage teaches us the value of resilience, resourcefulness, and the determination to overcome challenges. It's the foundation upon which we build our journey towards greater success and security.

Then comes Security. Here, you've got a bit more breathing room. You can cover your bills, you've got a place to call home, a car in the driveway, and maybe even a bit of savings. You're on a path to being income-independent; a few months without a regular paycheck won't send you into a panic. Getting your FUN Score figured out sooner rather than later means you'll have more time to enjoy the fruits of your labor with your loved ones.

It's easy to slip into the mindset of believing we have an unlimited amount of time ahead of us. But the truth is, we all have an expiration date on this journey called life. It's a shared reality that none of us can escape. So, while you're busy making plans, chasing dreams, and building your future, remember that time is a precious resource. Don't let the illusion of infinite time lull you into complacency. Seize the opportunities, cherish the moments, and make every day count. Because in the end, it's not about the quantity of time we have; it's about how we choose to make the most of it. Start taking steps towards your financial freedom today, so you can make the most of your time with those who matter most.

Next, the FUN (Freedom) stage, the part of the journey where life takes on an exhilarating twist. You've successfully taken care of your fundamental needs, and now you're setting your sights on the exciting extras that add spice to life. What makes this stage particularly captivating is the concept of financial freedom. Picture this: you've reached a point where your essential expenses are comfortably covered, and you're not merely dependent on active income from your day-to-day work. Instead, your lifestyle is fueled by passive income streams that you've cleverly set up along the way. This is the sweet spot where you get to call the shots and live life on your own terms.

Financial freedom in the FUN stage means that you've achieved a level of autonomy that many strive for, but few attain. You're no longer tied to the traditional 9 to 5 grind; you have the flexibility to explore new horizons, pursue your passions, and seize exciting opportunities without the constant pressure of financial obligations.

Imagine waking up every day with the freedom to choose how you spend your time. Whether it's embarking on a new adventure, dedicating more hours to a hobby you love, or simply relishing the joy of spending quality moments with your loved ones. Your financial stability is no longer a source of worry, and your decisions are guided by your desires and aspirations rather than financial constraints.

The FUN stage is not just about accumulating wealth; it's about intelligently channeling your resources into income-generating avenues that provide ongoing support for your chosen lifestyle. It's about leveraging your financial smarts to create a safety net that allows you to experience life in its full vibrancy.

As you journey through the FUN stage, keep in mind that achieving financial freedom requires careful planning, strategic investments, and a commitment to building diverse income streams. It's a thrilling chapter in your life story, one that empowers you to savor the freedom of choice and bask in the pleasures of life that truly matter to you. So, as you embark on this phase, remember that it's not just about the destination; it's about the thrilling adventure of financial liberation that lies ahead.

Last but not least, there's the Wealth stage. At this point, your perspective expands beyond just your own needs and desires. You're considering how your skills, knowledge, and resources can be harnessed to create a positive influence on the world around you. It's a remarkable phase where you're not only focused on personal success but also on contributing to the betterment of others and society as a whole. And here's an interesting twist: achieving this stage often brings the other three stages, Survival, Security, and FUN, into alignment as well.

The journey towards wealth is a transformational one. It signifies a shift from a self-centric outlook to a broader, more inclusive viewpoint. You're not just accumulating wealth for the sake of it; you're looking for ways to utilize your abundance to leave a meaningful mark on the world. It could involve philanthropy, mentorship, or creating products and services that address pressing issues.

As you navigate the path to wealth, remember that it's not just about amassing financial assets. It's about cultivating a mindset that recognizes the potential for positive change that comes with financial prosperity. By reaching the Wealth stage, you're not only securing your own future but also actively shaping the future of others.

Interestingly, the journey to wealth often acts as a catalyst, propelling the other dimensions, Survival, Security, and FUN, to new heights. When you're committed to making a positive impact, you naturally become more resourceful, focused, and resilient. This, in turn, enhances your ability to overcome challenges, secure your financial well-being, and enjoy the freedom to pursue your passions.

So, as you embark on the journey towards the Wealth stage, keep in mind the interconnected nature of these dimensions. By striving for wealth with a purpose-driven mindset, you're not just elevating your own life but also creating a ripple effect of positive transformation that enriches the lives of those around you.

Sometimes we find ourselves getting stuck in the frustration of the present moment. Instead, let's shift that focus to the future. It's like seeing the bigger picture. So, in this book, we're diving deep into building that FUN number, the magic spot where you're truly living life to the fullest.

Reaching Your FUN Score in 4 Simple Steps

1. Determine Your Dreams: Take the time to identify what you truly want in life. Clarify your goals and aspirations to create a clear direction for your future.
2. Put It in Writing: Document your goals and dreams. Writing them down helps solidify your commitment and serves as a roadmap for your journey ahead.
3. Find a Guide: Seek guidance and support to help you navigate the path towards your goals. Whether it's a mentor, coach, or advisor, having a blueprint crafted by someone experienced can accelerate your progress.
4. Take Action Daily: Consistency is key. Commit to taking small steps towards your goals every day. By consistently working towards your aspirations, you'll steadily move closer to reaching your FUN Score.

The Main Management Skills Needed for Success

- Management of cash flow
- Management of expenditure
- Management of profits

The CLEAR Pathway to Financial Understanding

Let's talk about clarity, the kind you need in both money matters and leadership. Just like how your car windshield can get all messed up with rain, dirt, and bugs, your financial and leadership vision can get cloudy too. Imagine driving in the rain with a windshield covered in gunk. You can't see well, and it's risky. The same goes for leadership. If your vision is unclear, you might end up making mistakes just like that driver would.

Leaders need a clear vision, just like a driver needs a clean windshield. Without it, they might crash into obstacles on their way to success. Think about it, if you can't see clearly, you won't know which steps to take.

That's where the CLEAR pathway comes in:
- C stands for Cost: that's your spending.
- L stands for Liabilities: the stuff you owe, like loans.
- E stands for Equity: what you own, like a house.
- A stands for Assets: your stuff, like savings or a rental property.
- R stands for Revenue: that's your earnings.

Using the CLEAR pathway is like putting on a pair of clear glasses. It helps you see your finances and leadership without any confusing stuff in the way. Just like cleaning your car windshield, it makes everything much clearer. Following the CLEAR pathway, YOU can navigate the world of financial literacy with confidence, making informed decisions about assets, liabilities, equity, revenue, and costs. Let's embark on this journey to financial empowerment together!

Have you ever heard the saying, Bees don't waste their time explaining to flies that honey is better than manure? It might sound a bit funny, but there's a brilliant lesson hidden in those quirky words, especially when it comes to learning business acumen.

Picture this, Bees are like the experts of the business world, buzzing around and creating sweet, valuable honey. They know how to work together, make smart decisions, and turn their efforts into something amazing. On the other hand, flies might just hang around, well, you know, not really contributing much and not understanding the value of honey.

Let's relate this to your journey of learning business acumen. Think of honey as the sweet success you want to achieve in the world of business. It's financial freedom, making smart investments, and turning your ideas into something incredible. Flies, well, they might represent those who don't really understand how business works or don't take the time to learn.

Increasing your business acumen is like being a bee. It's about understanding the ins and outs of how businesses run, how money flows, and how to make smart decisions that lead to sweet results. When you have business expertise, you're equipped with the knowledge and skills to create your own path, make wise choices, and turn your efforts into something valuable, just like bees turning flowers into honey.

So, why bother learning about business? Because just like bees know that honey is way better than poop (yep, flies might not get that), you'll know that understanding how business works is way better than staying in the dark. It's about seizing opportunities, making the right moves, and building a future that's as sweet as honey. So, dive into the world of business, and get ready to create your very own hive of success!

Understanding the Difference Between Busy Work and Success

If you've ever felt like you're constantly running on the hamster wheel of life, trying to achieve financial success but feeling like you're not making real progress, you're not alone. It's like hiking up a mountain. Some paths are clear, some are rocky, and, well, some just lead you in circles. That's where we'll start today; understanding the difference between being genuinely productive and just being busy.

First off, let's tackle the age-old confusion: busy work ≠ success. Just because your day is packed from sunup to sundown doesn't mean you're necessarily moving forward. Let's dive in.

The Busy Work Trap

Busy work is like junk food; it gives the illusion of satisfaction without any real sustenance. You might feel productive because you've ticked off 20 items on your to-do list, but were those tasks truly pushing you towards your financial goals? Or were they just keeping you busy?

Here are some classic signs you might be caught in the busy work trap:

- You're always "busy" but not richer or closer to your financial targets.
- You're overwhelmed but can't pinpoint tangible outcomes from your efforts.
- You often say "I just don't have the time" when confronted with real opportunities.

To move from busy work to meaningful work, consider these principles:

- Set clear goals: Know exactly what financial success looks like for you.
- Prioritization: Not every task is of equal importance. Determine which tasks can have the most impact.
- Time for Strategy: Instead of being reactive, take time to think, plan, and strategize your next moves.

So, how do you shift from a busy work mindset to a meaningful one? Remember, being constantly busy might give you the illusion of progress, but true financial success is built on intentional, strategic steps forward. So, next time you feel overwhelmed by your to-do list, take a moment to ask yourself, "Is this busy work or am I genuinely moving closer to my goals?"

Identifying Roadblocks to Achieving Financial Freedom

One afternoon, a daughter confided in her father about how her life was constantly filled with struggles and sorrows. She felt weary from the ongoing battles and challenges that seemed to emerge one after another. Her father listened intently. After some time passed, they found themselves in the kitchen. Her father began filling three pots with water and placing them on a high flame. As the water in the pots came to a boil, he added potatoes to one, eggs to another, and ground coffee beans to the third.

The daughter was so engrossed in her story that the sun had begun to set. Then he turned off the burners and proceeded to empty the contents of each pot into separate containers. Potatoes, eggs, and coffee sat in their respective containers. With a smile, her father asked, "What do you see?"

"Potatoes, eggs, and coffee," she replied. He handed her a cup of coffee and encouraged her to take a sip. The aroma filled the air, and a smile appeared on her face. Puzzled, the daughter asked, "What's the meaning behind all this, Dad?"

Her father went on to explain the profound lesson embedded within this simple kitchen experiment. The potatoes, eggs, and coffee beans faced the same challenge; boiling water. However, their reactions were vastly different. The potato, although strong initially, grew weak and softened when subjected to boiling water. The egg, with its delicate shell, turned hard on the inside after being exposed to the heat. The coffee beans, however, transformed the water itself, changing it into something entirely new.

Her father asked gently, "Which one are you? When life's difficulties come knocking, do you respond like the potato, the egg, or the coffee bean?"

Life presents challenges to everyone. How we respond to those challenges defines our character and outcome. Just like the coffee beans, we can choose to transform difficult situations into something positive and empowering. The story encourages us to actively choose our response to challenges, fostering a mindset of strength and positivity. We possess the power to influence our thoughts, decisions, and actions despite external circumstances. Instead of succumbing to difficulties, we can utilize them to catalyze personal growth and positive change.

We all can shape our own narrative. When faced with adversity, we can either weaken, harden, or transform. By choosing a perspective that aligns with the coffee beans, we can navigate life's challenges, create positive change, and inspire others along the way.

Elevating Self-Worth for Success

The most common stumbling block that hinders both business and personal growth are the stories we tell ourselves. Every person has a narrative, a story they've built around their struggles and challenges. They often share this story with others, highlighting the hardships and difficulties they've faced. But here's the twist: constantly reiterating these stories reinforces the idea that happiness, success, abundance, fulfilling relationships, and good health are out of their reach.

Your self-worth has an undeniable impact on your potential. It dictates the heights you can reach and the opportunities you can seize. But the path to higher self-worth isn't always a smooth one. It involves facing the uncomfortable truths and confronting the demons that lurk in your past, your experiences, and your psyche. It means diving back into the Shell, that place where memories and traumas reside, and dealing with them head-on. It's not easy, and it's not painless, but it's essential.

As you journey through this process of self-discovery and healing, something remarkable begins to unfold. You'll notice that your self-worth, once hindered by the weight of self-doubt, starts to expand. It grows, ever so slowly, as you shed the layers of unworthiness that held you back. And with every step, you free yourself from the limitations you once imposed upon yourself.

With increased self-worth, your perspective shifts. No longer will you settle for less, not in conversations, not in your thoughts, and certainly not in your actions. The negative thoughts that once plagued you lose their grip, replaced by newfound confidence and assurance.

You realize that the journey to self-worth is a universal one, a shared struggle that unites us all beneath the surface.

So, if you're wondering how to elevate your self-worth, remember that it's a journey of introspection, healing, and growth. The pains of the past may resurface, but they're steppingstones towards a higher, more empowered self. And as your self-worth rises, you'll find that your life begins to shift in remarkable ways, reaching heights you never thought possible.

Have you ever heard of the legendary katsuobushi? It's a fish so incredibly tough that even a knife can't cut through it. It all starts from the delicate meat of the bonito fish. Through a rigorous process of smoking and aging, this fish undergoes a radical transformation, emerging as something truly remarkable, resilient, and solid. Imagine a fish with a toughness that even a sharp knife finds hard to crack. This fish is so sturdy that you could use it as a hammer in a pinch. And get this some creative minds have actually turned it into a knife!

Let's apply this concept to business and personal growth. Just like the katsuobushi fish transforms into something unexpectedly sturdy, we too can go through remarkable transformations. Through challenges, experiences, and learning, we can develop an unshakable resilience and strength that surprises even ourselves. Much like the katsuobushi, we can evolve into tools of unexpected utility, navigating tough situations with unwavering determination and creativity.

So, remember, even in the face of challenges, we have the potential to become as unyielding as the katsuobushi. Our growth journey molds us into something remarkable, equipped to handle whatever comes our way. Just like the katsuobushi's journey from tender flesh to unbreakable strength, our journey through life and business can shape us into forces to be reckoned with.

It's time to let go of the narratives that hold us back and realize that we're in control. We have the pen, and we can start scripting a narrative that aligns with our aspirations and potential. As we release the hold of the past and embark on the journey of self-discovery and self-improvement, we pave the way for a new chapter that's brimming with possibilities. So, rather than being constrained by the stories we've clung to, let's take charge, embrace growth, and create a story that empowers us to achieve the success, happiness, and fulfillment we desire.

CHAPTER FIVE

Choices & The Ability To Harness Your Inner Superpowers

Have you ever noticed that villains and heroes often share a similar origin story? It's like they're cut from the same cloth, yet their paths diverge drastically. Let's take a closer look at how these backstories unfold and the critical role pain plays in shaping destinies. Villains and heroes, beneath their contrasting personas, start from a place of pain. Their backstories often involve loss, tragedy, or hardship. This common thread of pain binds them together at the start. If you pay attention to the details, you'll notice that screenwriters and storytellers drop hints in the form of scars, physical impairments, or unique speech patterns for villains. These aren't just random quirks; they're symbolic of their painful past.

The villain's choice, however, is to respond to that pain with vengeance. They declare, "The world hurt me, so I'll hurt it back." This decision sets them on a path of darkness and conflict. On the other side of the spectrum, the hero's response to pain is starkly different. Their backstory might be just as painful, but they choose to respond with courage and determination. Instead of seeking revenge, the hero declares, "The world hurt me, and I won't let this happen to others." This choice propels them into a journey of growth, self-discovery, and ultimately, triumph.

It's fascinating how pain is the common ground that villains and heroes share. It's a universal experience that touches us all. But here's the key takeaway: pain doesn't define us; our response to it does. Whether we become a villain or a hero in our own life story hinges on how we react to the challenges we face. This dynamic between pain, choices, and outcomes isn't limited to fictional worlds; it's a reflection of reality. Just like the villain and hero, we encounter pain in our lives. We all have our scars and stories of adversity. But we have the power to shape our narrative. Will we let pain consume us and turn us into villains of our own stories, seeking retribution? Or will we channel that pain into something greater, something heroic?

In business and life, the choice is ours. One path leads to the realm of villains, where setbacks define us negatively, and the other leads to heroism. Every challenge we face can be an opportunity for growth, transformation, and positive change. When setbacks come knocking, will we allow them to define us negatively, or will we choose to rise above and emerge as the heroes of our own stories? The lesson here is clear, it's not about what happens to us, but how we respond. So, when life throws its curveballs, remember that you hold the pen to your own narrative. The pain is shared, but the path is yours to decide. It's not about what life throws at us, but how we respond to what truly matters. Will you be the villain or the hero of your story?

Harnessing Your Inner Superpowers

Let's dive into your hidden arsenal of superpowers, the very tools that empower you to navigate life's twists, excel in the business arena, and make a meaningful impact.

Emotional Intelligence (EQ): Think of EQ as your empathy engine, your guiding light through social interactions. It's your ability to comprehend your emotions and understand the feelings of others. EQ enables you to forge authentic connections, manage conflicts, and lead with empathy. By harnessing EQ, you become a master at building relationships and navigating complex social dynamics.

Financial Intelligence (FQ): Meet your inner financial genius. FQ is all about mastering the language of money. It's about making sound financial decisions, understanding investment strategies, and ensuring that your hard-earned money works for you. With FQ, you're equipped to create wealth, secure your financial future, and wield control over your financial destiny.

- Social Intelligence (SQ): SQ is your social Swiss Army knife, helping you excel in any social situation. It's your knack for reading people, adapting to diverse environments, and communicating effectively. With SQ, you become a skilled communicator, a natural leader, and a networker extraordinaire. Your SQ is the key to thriving in teamwork, leadership, and relationship-building.
- Adversity Intelligence (AQ): Your resilience superhero steps onto the stage. AQ is your inner strength, your ability to face challenges head-on, and your capacity to bounce back from setbacks stronger than before. It's about viewing obstacles as steppingstones and embracing adversity as a catalyst for growth. AQ equips you to thrive in the face of adversity and transform difficulties into triumphs.
- Intelligence Quotient (IQ): Finally, there's the evergreen IQ, your cognitive powerhouse. IQ represents your ability to think critically, solve problems, and absorb new information. It's the foundation of your knowledge and intellectual development, enabling you to learn, adapt, and innovate.

These superpowers aren't isolated; they work in harmony, just like a symphony of talents. Successful individuals understand this synergy. They wield EQ to navigate relationships, apply FQ to financial endeavors, draw on SQ for social prowess, tap into AQ to overcome obstacles, and leverage IQ to make informed decisions.

And here's the thrilling part, these superpowers aren't exclusive to one domain. You can wield them in both your personal life and your professional pursuits. As you nurture your emotional intelligence, refine your financial acumen, enhance your social finesse, strengthen your resilience, and expand your intellectual horizons, you're shaping a roadmap to success.

Your mission, should you choose to accept it, is to harness these superpowers to the fullest. Cultivate your strengths, work on areas that need growth, and maintain a delicate balance among your EQ, FQ, SQ, AQ, and IQ. Embrace your uniqueness and remember that success is a symphony of these powers working in tandem. So, the adventure begins. Unleash your superpowers and set your course for soaring success.

Being Right vs. Feeling Right

In life and business, we often find ourselves navigating through decisions and situations with the instinct to be right. We rely on our thoughts, gut feelings, and past experiences to guide us. Just like a pilot flying in challenging conditions, we use our internal instruments to orient ourselves to the world around us.

Our feelings play a significant role in our decision-making process. We want to be right, and the main way we gauge this is by feeling right. However, relying solely on our feelings can be complicated and risky. Unlike a pilot's instruments that are reliable, our feelings can easily get mis calibrated. Our gut feelings are influenced by our biases and emotions. They are loyal to represent us as good and realistic, but they can lead us astray. We may believe that our gut is not biased, but it's essential to acknowledge that we all have biases and blind spots.

The human condition brings an irony that our feelings feel more factual than facts themselves. Our gut can be intensely convincing, making us believe our feelings even when faced with contrary evidence. Just like pilots flying with fallible instruments, we can sustain the sense of being on track even when we are off track.

Recognizing the difference between being right and feeling right is crucial. Many people believe they are exceptions to biases, falling into the bias blind spot. They think they are less biased and more rational than others. However, we must acknowledge that our thinking and talking are also influenced by our emotions and self-perception.

Being right takes effort. It requires careful analysis, consideration of evidence, and openness to new information. On the other hand, feeling right is easy. We can declare that we make good decisions based on our feelings alone, without the rigorous work of being right.

To make sound decisions in life and business, we must strike a balance between our emotions and rational thinking. It's essential to be aware of our biases and be open to challenging our assumptions. Just like a pilot relies on various instruments to ensure safety, we should use a combination of rational thinking, self-reflection, and input from others to make informed and successful choices. Being right might take more effort, but it's worth it to avoid the pitfalls of feeling right and ensuring long-term success and fulfillment in life and business.

Shifting from Being Right to Understanding

In both life and business, the pattern of obsessively needing to be right can be pervasive and destructive. Often, we get so wrapped up in defending our perspectives and opinions that we fail to consider the impact of this behavior on ourselves and others. This tendency to prioritize being right over understanding can lead to conflicts, damaged relationships, and flawed decisions.

When we operate from a posture of trying to be right, we approach situations with resistance and defensiveness. We hold onto our opinions firmly, creating a rigid and closed-off mindset. This defensive thinking is driven by a fear of being wrong, and it can cloud our judgment and decision-making process. As a result, we may become reactive and irrational, focusing more on winning arguments than finding common ground.

In both personal and professional settings, trying to be right can hinder collaboration and cooperation. It can lead to closed communication and defensive responses from others, causing them to feel unheard and resistant. This approach pushes people away instead of drawing them closer.

On the other hand, when we choose to operate from a posture of understanding, we suspend judgment and defensiveness. We approach situations with openness, curiosity, and exploration. By seeking to understand, we create an environment where others feel safe and valued. This fosters better communication, increased trust, and a willingness to cooperate.

Understanding requires us to be present and aware of our biases and fears. It involves recognizing our patterns of trying to be right and consciously shifting our approach to one of empathy and active listening. When we try to understand, we become more compassionate and willing to explore different viewpoints. This opens up possibilities for growth, innovative solutions, and deeper connections.

In life and business, shifting from the need to be right to the intention to understand is a powerful and transformative step. It enables us to build stronger relationships, make better decisions, and create a more inclusive and supportive environment. By embracing a posture of understanding, we can navigate challenges with clarity and resilience, ultimately leading to greater success and fulfillment in both personal and professional realms.

Reframing Negative Thoughts About Money

Ever catch those sneaky negative thoughts about money sneaking into your mind? We all do it from time to time. But here's a clever trick to show those thoughts who's boss! When you catch yourself thinking, "I'll never save enough cash," hit the pause button and flip the script. Try this on for size, "I've got what it takes to save money and build a solid financial foundation." It's like a quick mindset makeover that boosts your confidence and guides you toward better choices. Let's dive into those pesky negative thoughts we often have about money. We'll give them a run for their money by showing how a simple perspective shift can create more positive results:

Negative Thought: "I don't make enough money to save."

- Reframe: "I can start small and gradually increase my savings. Every little bit counts, and over time, it will add up to financial security."

Negative Thought: "Money only causes problems."

- Reframe: "Money is a tool that can be used to create opportunities and improve our lives. It's how we manage and prioritize it that determines its impact."

Negative Thought: "It's more difficult to get rich these days."

- Reframe: "The modern world offers numerous avenues for wealth creation, and with dedication, innovation, and smart decisions, I can achieve financial success."

Negative Thought: "I'll never pay off my school loans."

- Reframe: "By creating a realistic repayment plan and making consistent efforts to pay off my loans, I will eventually free myself from the burden of debt."

Negative Thought: "I'm never going to understand investing; why bother?"

- Reframe: "Investing may seem complex, but I can educate myself and seek guidance from financial experts to make informed decisions for my future."

Negative Thought: "I'll never make as much money as so-and-so."

- Reframe: "Comparing myself to others is counterproductive. Instead, I'll focus on my unique skills and strengths, and how I can maximize my potential."

Negative Thought: "I can only make so much money in my chosen field."

- Reframe: "While my current field may have its limitations, I can explore new opportunities, acquire new skills, or start a side business to increase my income."

Negative Thought: "I'm too old to start saving for retirement."

- Reframe: "It's never too late to begin saving for retirement. I can make a solid financial plan and take steps now to secure a comfortable future."

Negative Thought: "You need money to make money."

- Reframe: "While having capital helps, there are creative ways to start a business or invest with little money. I can leverage my skills and networks to grow."

Negative Thought: "Money isn't that important."

- Reframe: "Money plays a significant role in achieving my goals and providing security for my loved ones. Embracing its importance will lead to better decisions."

Negative Thought: "I'm not checking my credit card balance because I don't want to know."

Reframe: "Facing my finances head-on empowers me to take control and make positive changes. I will monitor my spending and manage debt responsibly."

Negative Thought: "I've made too many money mistakes to ever recover."

- Reframe: "Past mistakes are opportunities to learn and grow. I will use them as lessons to make better choices and create a brighter financial future."

Remember, a simple shift in perspective can turn those negative money thoughts into positive actions. So, the next time those thoughts start creeping in, give them a run for their money and watch how your financial outlook transforms for the better!

Unveiling the Hidden Key to Financial Freedom: Taxes

Have you ever stopped to think about one of the most overlooked expenses? It's not something you see immediately, but it impacts everyone, especially those who might be struggling financially. What's this hidden cost? It's taxes. And guess what? It affects the wealthy and the poor alike. But here's where the plot thickens and a secret to financial success is revealed.

You see, the wealthy have a unique insight into the world of income, and it's not what you might think. They've figured out that the number one expense for most people, which is taxes, can be managed strategically. And that's where their journey toward financial freedom takes a significant turn.

Mastering the Tax Game

Let's break down taxes in a way that's as clear as day. Imagine you have a crisp dollar bill in your hand, that's your hard-earned money. Now, get ready to see how taxes can impact it.

In the active income corner, when you make that dollar through a job or similar means, your biggest expense is none other than taxes. Picture this: out of that dollar, around 40 cents goes straight into the tax bucket. So, what do you have left? About 60 cents that you get to keep.

Let's switch gears to the passive income arena. This is where things get interesting. With passive income, like certain investments, the tax game changes. Imagine having that same dollar, but this time earned passively. The good news? You might get to keep the entire dollar or be taxed way less than before. We're talking around a mere 20 cents.

Now, think about it for a moment. With active income, you end up with 60 cents after taxes. But with smart passive income choices, you could be looking at keeping that whole dollar or having around 80 cents in your pocket after taxes. Quite the difference, right?

It's like you're discovering the secret passageways in the tax maze. The more you understand and utilize passive income opportunities, the more you can potentially keep in your own pocket.

So, here's the takeaway. Knowing the tax rules can make a huge impact on your financial journey. By leaning into passive income options, you're not just earning money; you're playing the tax game with some serious strategy.

Remember, it's not about being a tax expert overnight. It's about realizing that active and passive income play by different tax rules. And when you choose investments or avenues that offer those sweet tax benefits, you're stepping into the world of financial intelligence.

So, whether you're aiming to keep that entire dollar or maximize what you take home, remember this lesson in taxes. It's your money, after all why not make sure you're holding onto as much of it as possible?

Boost Your FUN Score with Smart Investment Choices

Hey there, savvy investor! Today, let's dive into something that could give your FUN Score a serious boost. We're talking about investments, but don't worry this won't be a jargon-heavy lecture. We're keeping it simple and straightforward.

Think of investments as puzzle pieces that contribute to your overall financial picture. You might have heard about dividend stocks, bonds, cryptocurrency, real estate, and even tangible items like cars and boats. They all have something in common: they can potentially bring you more money down the line. But here's the catch taxes. When you sell an investment, there's something called capital gains tax that comes into play. Now, capital gains tax might sound a bit intimidating, but it's essentially a tax on the profit you make from selling something that's gained value over time.

Now, here's the cool part. Not all gains are created equal. Some investments, like most dividend stocks, fall under the category of "qualified dividends." Why does this matter? Because qualified dividends are taxed at a rate that can range from a super-friendly 0% all the way to a still very reasonable 20%.

Here's where the magic happens. Compare this range to the tax rates you'd face for your regular income; those can be anywhere from 10% to a much higher 37% or even more. See the difference? The 0% to 20% range for qualified dividends looks like a tax party you'd want to join, right?

Now, you might be wondering where you fit into all this tax talk. That's where a quick online search comes in. With just a few clicks, you can find out how these tax rates apply to your specific situation. Here's the bottom line: by understanding the tax advantages of certain investments like qualified dividends, you're taking a step toward boosting your FUN Score. Think about it not only are you making smart investment choices, but you're also keeping more of your money thanks to those favorable tax rates.

This isn't just about numbers on a screen. It's about making choices that impact your financial future. And by exploring investments with these tax benefits, you're setting yourself up for success.

So, give yourself a pat on the back for diving into this topic. Armed with this knowledge, you're better equipped to make informed decisions that align with your financial goals. Your FUN Score is all about making the right moves, and understanding taxes in the investment game is a serious game-changer.

A Lazy Man Works Twice as Hard

Applying these positive reframes in personal, professional, marital, and parenting contexts will empower individuals to take charge of their financial well-being, make informed decisions, and create a harmonious and prosperous life. By embracing a business mindset in these areas, individuals can develop strategies for success, optimize resources, and foster a sense of accomplishment and fulfillment in every endeavor.

Lazy Legs work twice as hard! Let me share a tale about a young boy who had quite the lazy streak. It was a sunny day, much like any other, and his mother, wise woman that she was, often reminded him, "Do your best work always! Remember, a lazy man works twice as hard." Now, this boy would just brush off her words with a grin, thinking he had it all figured out.

One day, his mother asked him to take out the trash. Instead of walking down the stairs to the garbage can, he had a bright idea. He decided to toss the bag out the window, assuming it would land perfectly in the can below. But alas, fate had other plans. The bag missed its mark, burst open upon landing, and garbage was thrown everywhere.

As he made his way downstairs, he faced an unpleasant scene of trash scattered about the yard. His mother, having witnessed the whole spectacle, shook her head in disappointment. "A lazy man works twice as hard," she sighed, a touch of disapproval in her voice.

Feeling embarrassed and realizing his blunder, the lad finally grasped the wisdom behind his mother's words. He sighed, rolled up his sleeves, and got to work. He worked more than twice as hard, expending the effort he would've needed if he'd just taken the trash down properly. Picking up each piece of litter, he felt the weight of his own laziness. And that day marked a turning point. He realized that laziness only led to more work in the end. "A lazy man works twice as hard," he muttered to himself, a valuable lesson learned.

This lesson holds true in life and business. It's like the philosophical notion of knowledge avoidance and willful ignorance both leading to irrational reasoning patterns. Let's explore how avoiding responsibility and personal autonomy in four vital aspects health, parenting, finances, and faith can impact us.

When we dodge taking charge of our health, we might ignore medical needs and put our well-being at risk. This can result in delayed diagnoses and missed chances for preventive care, ultimately affecting our quality of life. Similarly, in parenting, shirking responsibility can hinder effective nurturing and guidance. Without actively engaging and owning our parenting choices, our children might miss out on the support and structure they need to grow.

In matters of money, avoiding ownership can lead to financial chaos. Not facing financial planning can result in debt, limited growth, and missed chances for stability and wealth accumulation. Lastly, ignoring our beliefs can lead to a superficial understanding of spirituality and morality. Refusing to engage might leave us without a deep sense of purpose.

The impact of avoiding these responsibilities is clear missed opportunities for growth and well-being. By embracing autonomy, we unlock doors to self-improvement. Owning our health means healthier living. Taking active roles in parenting fosters strong family bonds. Facing our financial matters leads to stability and growth. Engaging with faith brings meaning and understanding.

In a nutshell, dodging knowledge and willful ignorance can hinder growth and rational thinking. By embracing responsibility in health, parenting, finances, and faith, we open up possibilities for positive outcomes and fulfillment. Taking control empowers us to make informed decisions, leading to a more meaningful life journey. Just remember, a lazy approach might make you work twice as hard in the end.

Guiding Instead of Pushing: A Path to Encourage Growth

You know that feeling when someone's pushing you? It's uncomfortable, right? The same goes for kids and even for us as adults. Nobody likes being forced into something. Whether it's in life or business, the idea of pushing doesn't usually yield the best results.

Imagine a child you're trying to guide. When you're standing behind them, pushing them forward, they often resist. It's natural, really. Now, flip that scenario. Instead of pushing, you hold their hand and gently lead them. They're much more receptive, right? It's the same for us. We prefer being pulled towards something rather than being pushed.

The same concept applies to businesses. If you're always pushing your employees or customers, they might push back or feel reluctant. But if you take the time to guide, support, and create an environment where they want to engage, it's a game-changer.

See, pulling, leading, and guiding are like creating a lifestyle. You're making it so appealing that people naturally want to follow. In life, this means offering guidance and support rather than trying to force decisions. In business, it's about fostering an environment where everyone is inspired to be part of the journey. When you pull people in with genuine care and a clear vision, you'll be amazed at how much further you can go together.

Remember, lead instead of pushing, and guide instead of forcing. It's not just about getting someone to do something; it's about inspiring them to want to do it. Whether it's in your personal life or your business endeavors, this approach can lead to more genuine engagement, growth, and success.

Navigating Stress for Enhanced Focus

Hey there! Let's dive into something that affects us all, stress! You know those moments when you feel like your mind is all over the place? That's what we call being scatterbrained. It's like your attention is a butterfly, flitting from one thing to another. But did you know this can mess with your focus and even ramp up your stress levels? Take a moment to think about how it feels when your thoughts are all over the map. It's like trying to juggle too many balls at once, and it's no surprise that this can stress you out, especially when you're fully aware that you're having trouble concentrating.

Let's talk about the good stuff. Understanding how this all works and how it can level up your game in both life and business. When your focus is on point, you're like a laser beam, zeroing in on your tasks and nailing them one by one. But when stress enters the picture, it's like throwing a bunch of obstacles in your path. You're not only dealing with the challenges at hand but also the added weight of feeling scattered and unfocused.

So, how does understanding this help? Well, when you recognize that stress can mess with your focus, you're taking the first step toward managing it. By acknowledging the impact stress has on your ability to concentrate, you can start finding ways to combat it. Here's where the magic happens. When you find effective ways to handle stress whether it's through deep breathing, exercise, meditation, or simply taking breaks you'll notice something incredible. Your focus starts to sharpen, and you become more efficient in tackling tasks. With less stress pulling you in all directions, you'll find it easier to stay on track and get things done.

Let's apply this insight to both life and business. In your personal life, think about how much smoother things can run when you're focused. Quality time with loved ones becomes truly meaningful. You're able to engage fully in activities you enjoy, soaking up every moment without distractions pulling you away. In the business realm, honing your focus is a game-changer. Imagine the difference it makes when you're able to concentrate deeply on your projects. You're more productive, innovative ideas flow more freely, and you're better equipped to tackle challenges head-on.

In the hustle and bustle of life, there's something truly remarkable about being present in the moment. It's like hitting the pause button on the chaos and fully immersing yourself in what's happening right now. Let's explore this concept further how it can elevate your experiences and how it applies to both life and business.

Think about it—have you ever started your workday before even reaching the office? Maybe while you were still in the shower or at the breakfast table? It's a common occurrence, and it can mess with your focus and productivity. You end up mentally split between different places, and that's not productive at all. Even when you're at the beach, your mind might be wandering back to the office, creating a loop of distraction.

Now, imagine a different scenario. Imagine committing to being fully present in the current moment, no matter where you are. Whether you're having breakfast, chatting with a friend, or on your way to work, be there completely. It's like giving your undivided attention to whatever you're doing. Here's where the beauty lies. Being present not only enhances your experiences but also benefits you in unexpected ways. When you're fully engaged in the present, you're able to absorb everything around you, learn from it, and even find inspiration. You start noticing human nature, the small details, and the interactions that often go unnoticed.

Let's connect the dots and apply this principle to both life and business. In your personal life, being present deepens your connections. Picture yourself fully engaged in a conversation with someone. You're not half-listening while thinking about something else; you're actually there, in the moment. The bond you create becomes more authentic, and you gain a deeper understanding of others.

In the business realm, being present translates to heightened productivity and creativity. When you're in a meeting or working on a project, your focus is unwavering. You grasp ideas, collaborate effectively, and make decisions with clarity. This level of engagement sets you apart and fuels your success.

So, what's the life lesson here? It's simple yet profound; wherever you are, be there. It's about fully embracing the now, whether it's a quiet moment at home or a bustling day at the office. By practicing this, you'll find that life becomes richer, experiences become more meaningful, and success becomes more attainable.

In conclusion, being present is a skill that can transform the way you approach life and business. It's about cherishing every moment and harnessing its potential. Just like understanding how stress impacts focus, mastering the art of being present is another powerful tool in your arsenal. So, as you move through your day, remember this. Be present, be engaged, and watch as life unfolds in its most vibrant and rewarding form.

The lesson here is clear, understanding how stress can mess with your focus is your secret weapon. By recognizing this dynamic, you're taking control of your focus and, in turn, your effectiveness in both your personal and professional life. So, when you feel the stress creeping in and your focus waning, remember that you have the power to reclaim your attention and boost your performance. It's all about understanding, applying, and achieving the next level of focus and success.

Internal Adjustments

In various aspects of life, the challenges we encounter often find their roots within our own responses and choices. The key to overcoming these obstacles effectively lies in recognizing the need for introspection and making internal shifts. Through a series of scenarios, let's uncover the transformative potential of understanding and addressing our internal dynamics.

The Husband's Wake-Up Call and Active Parenthood

Consider a common scenario where a husband pretends to be asleep while his wife tends to the baby. The internal solution here is for him to embrace a shared responsibility mindset. Recognizing that parenthood is a team effort and actively participating in caregiving can strengthen family bonds and foster a more supportive and equal partnership.

Confronting Workplace Avoidance and Taking Ownership

Imagine an individual avoiding addressing problems at work, hoping they will go away on their own. The internal fix for this situation involves cultivating a sense of accountability and proactiveness. Understanding that unresolved issues can impact team dynamics and overall productivity can empower them to speak up and contribute to finding solutions.

Shattering Assumptions at Work and Fostering Collaboration

Let's discuss the "it's not my job" mentality that can hinder collaboration in the workplace. The internal adjustment required here is to adopt a proactive stance. By embracing the idea of collective responsibility and taking initiative to assist when needed, a more cooperative and supportive work environment can be cultivated.

Observation to Action and Being Accountable

Consider the individual on the ship who spots a problem but fails to take action. The internal solution in this case centers around understanding the value of responsibility and accountability. Embracing a proactive approach, even when the issue doesn't directly involve them, can make a significant impact in critical situations.

The Rule Maker's Transformation

Imagine the scenario of the "rule maker," the person who assigns tasks, creates rules, and sends memos and emails. Often, this individual appears busy and involved, but their accountability may be questionable. This situation calls for an internal adjustment that centers on accountability and authenticity.

A Shift Towards Accountability

In this scenario, the rule maker may appear to be engaged and productive, yet the true essence of accountability is missing. The internal fix involves recognizing the difference between being genuinely helpful and merely appearing busy. Understanding that true accountability goes beyond delegating tasks and extends to taking responsibility for the outcomes is pivotal.

The Power of Authentic Engagement

The rule maker needs to shift from superficial busyness to genuine accountability. This means actively engaging with tasks, memos, and emails in a way that reflects true ownership. By taking responsibility for the impact of their decisions and actions, they contribute to a more efficient and harmonious work environment.

Inspiring Others

The internal adjustment required here is to recognize that leadership is not about dictating tasks but about fostering collaboration and accountability. By leading through example, the rule maker can inspire others to take ownership and contribute effectively. This collaborative approach leads to a more empowered and engaged team.

In the journey of leadership, one must never underestimate the profound influence of internal adjustments. When we shift our focus from mere delegation to embracing genuine accountability, an extraordinary transformation takes place. The rule maker, once a superficial contributor, evolves into an agent of impactful leadership. It's essential to keep in mind that leadership isn't solely defined by the tasks you delegate; rather, it's measured by the profound impact you have and the inspiration you instill in others.

As this internal shift takes root, the rule maker becomes equipped to lead with authenticity, responsibility, and an unwavering commitment to fostering positive change. By introspectively exploring these scenarios, we uncover a fundamental truth: personal and professional growth emanates from within. The ability to question our behaviors, beliefs, and attitudes emerges as a paramount force. Nurturing a mindset of responsibility, empathy, and proactive problem-solving empowers every individual to make positive contributions to relationships, work environments, and society as a whole.

Always remember that the genesis of change lies within us. Through these internal transformations, each person holds the potential to co-create a brighter and better world for everyone. It's a journey that begins from the depths of our own introspection and leads to the heights of collective progress.

CHAPTER SIX

MARRIAGE & PARTNERSHIP

Treating Marriage Like a Business: A Recipe for Lasting Love

Marriage and business may seem like two distinct worlds, but could they hold common ground? Let's explore how the principles that guide successful businesses can also contribute to building a lasting, fulfilling marriage.

Just as in business, finding a life partner requires careful consideration. It's like selecting a business partner; you're seeking someone who shares your values, supports your goals, and complements your strengths. Both in love and business, compatibility is key. Just as a business partnership can flourish with aligned visions, a marriage thrives when partners walk side by side toward a shared future.

Why compare marriage to business? Because the essence remains the same building a successful partnership. In marriage, it's about nurturing a bond that enhances both partners' lives. Just as a business partnership demands commitment, adaptability, and mutual growth, a marriage thrives when fueled by love, communication, and understanding.

In both realms, a commitment to support and understand one another is paramount. Imagine a business partnership where both parties are fully invested in each other's success. It's no different in marriage. When you choose a partner who's genuinely supportive and eager to collaborate, you create a foundation for mutual growth.

Just as a business's success hinges on delivering value to customers, a successful marriage thrives on meeting each other's needs. In business, value is delivered through products, services, and customer experiences that fulfill the client's needs and desires. Similarly, in marriage, value is delivered through emotional support, affection, and connection that nurture the relationship. This involves understanding what makes your partner feel loved, secure, and valued. For example, acts of kindness, words of affirmation, quality time, and physical affection are all ways to fulfill these emotional needs.

Consider the emotional landscape of a business. When promises are broken or commitments are not met, customers feel disappointed and frustrated, leading to a loss of trust and potential business. In marriage, the consequences of unmet emotional needs are just as significant. When one partner feels ignored, unsupported, or undervalued, it can lead to feelings of unhappiness, resentment, and emotional distance. For instance, if one partner consistently overlooks the other's need for quality time or fails to offer support during tough times, the relationship can suffer.

By treating marriage with the same seriousness and commitment as a business, you emphasize the importance of keeping promises and fulfilling commitments that contribute to the well-being of your partner and the relationship. This means actively listening to your partner's concerns, offering consistent support, and making efforts to show love and appreciation regularly. Just as a successful business adapts to changing customer needs and strives for continuous improvement, a thriving marriage involves ongoing effort to understand and meet each other's emotional needs. This creates a foundation of trust, mutual respect, and happiness, making the relationship a safe and supportive haven for both partners.

Effective communication, a cornerstone of business success, also plays a significant role in marriage. Sharing openly, listening actively, and working together toward shared goals strengthen the partnership. Just as a business thrives on teamwork, a marriage flourishes when both partners communicate openly and collaborate harmoniously. Flexibility and adaptability are other key aspects of both marriage and business. Just as a business evolves to meet market changes, a successful marriage adapts to personal growth and changing dynamics. Partners who support each other's individual development ensure the relationship remains strong and relevant.

The principles that guide a successful business partnership can be applied to building a strong and loving marriage. Just as successful businesses prioritize effective communication, mutual support, and meeting customers' needs, successful marriages thrive on open communication, fulfilling emotional needs, and nurturing a deep connection. By treating marriage with the same dedication, effort, and commitment as a business, partners can create a resilient and enduring bond that stands the test of time.

So, as you embark on the journey of love and partnership, consider the wisdom from the world of business. Approach marriage with intention, understanding, and a shared vision. By embracing these principles, you're not only building a loving relationship but also setting the stage for a lifelong partnership filled with growth, happiness, and fulfillment. Just as a business thrives under the right strategies, a marriage flourishes under the power of commitment, communication, and love.

Your Spouse and Financial Success

Picture this: your spouse as a co-pilot on your financial journey. Their actions and habits can either pave the way for your financial success or lead you down a rocky road. Let's dive into two stories that illustrate how a partner's financial behaviors can significantly impact your relationship, finances, and future.

Story 1: The Tennis Dress Dilemma

Once upon a time, a newly married woman and her friend embarked on a shopping expedition. The wife promised her husband that no purchases would be made, but temptation led her to buy an irresistible tennis dress on sale. Seems harmless, right? But this seemingly small action raised questions about respecting the family's financial boundaries and eroded trust between partners.

Story 2: The Golf Club Incident

In another corner of the world, a young couple navigated limited savings and financial aspirations. A disagreement emerged when the husband yearned for a day of golf with friends, despite the wife's financial concerns. In defiance of her wishes, he invested in an expensive golf club, igniting a chain reaction of financial conflicts that ultimately corroded their marriage.

These tales highlight a lesson, pay heed to your partner's financial behavior from the get-go. Early signs of financial friction can forecast future challenges. Keep an eye out for overspending tendencies, a fixation on materialism, or a disregard for financial planning. A supportive partner who values financial prudence can help lay the groundwork for a solid shared future.

Seek a partner open to financial growth, whether they're eager to learn or eager to teach. A supportive spouse will engage you in financial conversations, involve you in decision-making, and co-pilot financial discussions, investments, and savings. Take an active role in managing your financial ship together. Stay informed, contribute ideas, and be part of the financial journey that shapes your shared destiny.

Together, you can make well-informed investments, plan for tomorrow, and inspire each other to make smart financial choices. It all boils down to partnership, a blend of mutual encouragement, cooperation, and shared aspirations. Just as collaboration drives success in both life and business, your partnership in finances can set the stage for a prosperous future.

The Supportive Spouse: A Catalyst for Success

Imagine a driven entrepreneur at the helm of a thriving online marketing agency. Her sights are set on expanding the business by introducing specialized digital marketing courses and workshops. This exciting venture demands substantial investment in course materials, faculty, and marketing efforts.

With optimism comes caution, and she knows the risks attached to this new chapter. Seeking the input of a steadfast supporter, she shares her ambitious plans with him one evening. Over conversation, she articulates her vision, finding in him not just a listener but an enthusiast who rallies behind her ideas.

"I have absolute faith in you," he says with confidence. "Your marketing agency's success is proof enough. Your new courses will undoubtedly soar. I'm with you every step of the way."

His unshakeable support boosts her self-assurance. Guided by his financial and emotional backing, she embarks on this venture with newfound strength. A joint effort ensues as they devise budgets and financial projections. He contributes insights and suggestions, ensuring well-informed decisions. He even suggests leveraging their network to spread the word about the courses. As the launch approaches, he steps into a new role, managing household responsibilities to allow her more time to focus on her endeavor. He attends the inaugural workshop as a participant while offering constructive feedback for enhancement.

With him as her bedrock, her courses take the market by storm. The investment pays dividends, and the business expansion flourishes. Throughout, he remains her unwavering anchor. His cheers amplify her successes, and his encouragement helps navigate rough patches. Beyond business growth, their partnership blossoms.

The Power of a Supportive Life Partner

In certain parts of the world, like India, Pakistan, Japan, and China, arranged marriages have been a longstanding tradition. These cultures see arranged marriages as a way to bring families together, ensure compatibility, and uphold cultural norms. While this concept might be unfamiliar to many, there are valuable lessons to be learned from their success, which can be applied to both personal relationships and business partnerships.

Arranged marriages, prevalent in countries like India, boast divorce rates of less than 4 percent. This contrasts sharply with countries like the U.S., where the divorce rate hovers around 40 percent. What sets arranged marriages apart and contributes to their stability and longevity?

One possible explanation lies in the emphasis on compatibility and shared values. In arranged marriages, families play a significant role in selecting suitable partners, taking into account social status, religious beliefs, and financial background. This thorough process results in a foundation of common values and goals, which equips couples to navigate challenges and grow together.

Another factor is the strong support system that often accompanies arranged marriages. The extended family network provides valuable advice, guidance, and encouragement throughout the marriage journey. This sense of community ensures couples have access to a support system during both joyful and difficult times.

Arranged marriages also thrive due to the commitment and dedication of both partners. The collective decision to marry promotes a sense of responsibility and obligation to make the marriage work. This mutual investment in understanding each other's needs and resolving conflicts leads to long-term success.

This narrative shines a spotlight on the profound influence of support in both personal and professional spheres. When a partner believes in your dreams and champions your pursuits, it fuels the courage to chase ambitious goals. This united endeavor can yield remarkable triumphs and deep contentment across life's dimensions.

Pause and reflect. Is your partner your rock in both financial and personal endeavors? Imagine having a partner who supports and values your financial aspirations. Imagine sharing a vision for a secure future, someone who collaborates on budgets, discusses investments, and actively participates in building wealth. Now, envision a different scenario, one where financial differences or incompatibility hinder your growth. Consider the impact of misaligned financial values on your journey toward financial security. Your partner's support isn't just about their presence; it's about shared values and goals. It's about your joint ability to save, invest, and shape a future of prosperity.

Ultimately, choosing the right life partner can significantly shape your journey, both personally and in business. Building a financial foundation together sets the stage for a life infused with mutual success and lasting fulfillment. In unity, you discover the potential to soar beyond what you could achieve individually.

The lesson from arranged marriages extends beyond personal relationships; it's applicable to financial growth as well. The success of arranged marriages underscores the significance of compatibility and shared financial goals in a partnership. Just as couples in arranged marriages benefit from common values, achieving financial growth is easier when partners work toward shared financial objectives. Whether it's saving, investing, or managing debts, a united financial approach paves the way for stability and prosperity.

In both personal relationships and business partnerships, the lesson remains clear: building a strong and supportive partnership based on shared values, trust, and mutual understanding is crucial for growth. Just as arranged marriages stand as a testament to the value of compatibility and commitment, they also emphasize that a harmonious partnership is key to achieving both personal and financial success.

The Journey of Parenthood and Entrepreneurship: A Roller Coaster of Learning and Growth

Becoming a parent is similar to being an entrepreneur. Both have been a profound and transformative experience, much like embarking on an unpredictable roller coaster ride. The similarities between the two are striking, starting with the fact that you have no idea what you're in for until you're actually in it. Nothing could have prepared you for the challenges and joys that lie ahead.

Both roles come with their unique set of challenges, and those who haven't experienced them might struggle to understand the depth of your experiences. You may find yourself judged or receiving strange looks when you attempt to explain the intricacies of your journey. But there's no need to worry about others' understanding; what matters most is to accept and love yourself where you are on your path.

As a parent or an entrepreneur, you quickly learn the art of adaptation and embracing self-doubt, as both come with responsibilities like no other. You have to keep your baby and your business thriving, taking each step one at a time. Surrendering to the unknown becomes a valuable lesson as you trust in the bigger plan, understanding that life's course is beyond your control.

With each new child or venture, you become more experienced and find yourself better equipped to handle the challenges. Asking for help becomes second nature, as you learn that support is vital to success. Surrounding yourself with like-minded individuals who understand your journey becomes essential for growth and resilience.

Throughout the process, you come to understand that you're not alone in your experiences. Others have faced similar challenges and uncertainties, and like you, they learned to trust their intuition and take action. Imperfections become steppingstones, and failures are seen as opportunities to learn and improve.

As you continue to grow as a parent and an entrepreneur, you begin to value time as your most precious commodity. Embracing the present moment becomes crucial, understanding that love is the driving force behind both roles. Love for your children and clients propels you forward, encouraging you to celebrate their successes as if they were your own. Your attitude toward money changes as you see it as a means to an end rather than an end itself. Boundaries become vital in balancing your time and energy between family and business. In the face of desperation, you learn to have faith in yourself and your ability to thrive.

With time, you'll discover that leveraging time and resources becomes vital, finding ways to collaborate and seek help where needed. Laughter and playfulness become important elements in your journey, injecting joy and fun into your life.

Gratitude takes center stage as you appreciate the little things, like a peaceful shower, and the immense blessings of being a parent and entrepreneur. Your dreams grow more significant, encompassing the potential you see in the world.

The life you knew before embarking on these journeys becomes a distant memory, and you'll never look back. Parenthood and entrepreneurship are life-changing experiences that continually shape and mold you into a better version of yourself. Embrace the ride, be present in every moment, and celebrate the growth that comes with these remarkable roles.

Thriving in the Black as a Parent

As parents, our journey toward success often takes on a different hue, painted with the vibrant colors of love, growth, and fulfillment. While financial prosperity is undoubtedly important, true success as a parent transcends monetary measures. It's about fostering a nurturing environment where our children can flourish, guiding them toward a future filled with purpose and joy.

Success as a parent begins with laying a solid foundation of love and connection. It's about creating a warm and supportive home environment where our children feel cherished, valued, and accepted for who they are. It's in the moments spent cuddling on the couch, sharing laughter around the dinner table, and offering a comforting embrace during times of need.

But success in parenting goes beyond mere affection; it encompasses the art of teaching and guiding our children toward becoming compassionate, resilient, and independent individuals. It's about instilling in them a strong moral compass, teaching them the value of kindness, empathy, and integrity. It's in the lessons imparted through everyday interactions, where we model empathy, respect, and responsibility, shaping their character and guiding them toward making positive contributions to society.

Successful parenting also involves nurturing our children's passions and talents, encouraging them to explore their interests and pursue their dreams. It's about providing them with opportunities for growth and self-discovery, whether through extracurricular activities, educational experiences, or creative pursuits. It's in the moments of cheering from the sidelines, celebrating their achievements, and offering gentle encouragement during setbacks, empowering them to embrace their unique talents and reach their full potential.

Thriving in the Black as a parent also means finding balance and prioritizing self-care amongst the demands of parenthood. It's about recognizing that our well-being is intrinsically linked to the well-being of our children, and nurturing ourselves allows us to show up fully present and engaged for them. In moments of quiet reflection, embracing self-compassion, and reaching out for support from loved ones and communities, we replenish our spirits and foster our personal growth and fulfillment.

In essence, success as a parent is a journey defined by love, growth, and connection. It's about creating a nurturing environment where our children can thrive, guiding them toward becoming compassionate, resilient, and fulfilled individuals.

It's in the everyday moments of laughter, learning, and love, where the true richness of parenthood is found. And as we navigate this journey, may we find ourselves Thriving in the Black, both as parents and as individuals, embracing the joy and fulfillment that comes from nurturing the next generation with love and intentionality.

CHAPTER SEVEN

The Magical Rule of 72 Made Easy

Imagine you have a treasure chest filled with shiny gold coins. You want to know how long it will take for your treasure to double in value. Well, there's a magical rule that can help you figure it out, and it's called the Rule of 72. This rule is like a secret code that helps you understand how money grows over time. Let's dive in and uncover this treasure of knowledge!

The Rule of 72 is a special number that tells you approximately how many years it will take for your money to double when it's invested or earning interest. All you need to do is divide the number 72 by the interest rate. The result will be the number of years it takes for your money to double. For example, let's say you have a magic bank that gives you an interest rate of 6%. If you divide 72 by 6, you get 12. That means it will take around 12 years for your money to double in the bank.

Simple yet powerful, the best part about the Rule of 72 is that it's super easy to use and works for different interest rates. You don't need a calculator or a magic spell to figure it out. Just remember the number 72, and you're good to go!

Whether you're saving money in a piggy bank, putting it in a real bank, or even investing in the stock market, the Rule of 72 can give you a quick estimate of how your money will grow. It's like having a crystal ball!

Let's play with some numbers to see how cool the Rule of 72 really is. Imagine you have a wizardly investment that gives you an interest rate of 10%. If you divide 72 by 10, you get 7.2. That means in around 7.2 years, your money will double. So, if you start with 100 gold coins, in about 7.2 years, you'll have 200 gold coins! But what if you find an enchanted bank with an interest rate of 5%? Dividing 72 by 5 gives you 14.4. So, it will take around 14.4 years for your money to double at that bank.

The Rule of 72 is an important concept that helps us understand the power of compound interest. It tells us how long it takes for our money to double based on the interest rate we are earning. To determine this, simply divide 72 by the percent of interest you are earning. Albert Einstein once famously said, "Compound interest is the most powerful force in the universe." This statement emphasizes the remarkable impact that compound interest can have on our savings and investments over time.

Here are some examples to illustrate the Rule of 72:

Example 1: Growth at 0% Interest Rate

Age | Amount

0 | $1,000

10 | $1,000

20 | $1,000

30 | $1,000

40 | $1,000

50 | $1,000

60 | $1,000

70 | $1,000

Example 2: Growth at 3% Interest Rate

Age | Amount

0 | $1,000

10 | $1,430 (approximately doubles in 24 years)

20 | $2,043 (approximately doubles in 24 years)

30 | $2,917 (approximately doubles in 24 years)

40 | $4,174 (approximately doubles in 18 years)

50 | $5,956 (approximately doubles in 20 years)

60 | $8,512 (approximately doubles in 22 years)

70 | $12,140 (approximately doubles in 26 years)

Example 3: Growth at 6% Interest Rate

Age | Amount

0 | $1,000

10 | $1,791 (approximately doubles in 12 years)

20 | $3,207 (approximately doubles in 12 years)

30 | $5,743 (approximately doubles in 12 years)

40 | $10,287 (approximately doubles in 12 years)

50 | $18,405 (approximately doubles in 14 years)

60 | $32,886 (approximately doubles in 16 years)

70 | $58,828 (approximately doubles in 18 years)

Example 4: Growth at 12% Interest Rate

Age | Amount

0 | $1,000

10 | $3,106 (approximately doubles in 6 years)

20 | $9,646 (approximately doubles in 6 years)

30 | $29,957 (approximately doubles in 6 years)

40 | $93,045 (approximately doubles in 6 years)

50 | $289,425 (approximately doubles in 6 years)

60 | $899,084 (approximately doubles in 6 years)

70 | $2,797,691 (approximately doubles in 6 years)

Please note that these values are approximate and do not take into account compounding periods, fees, or taxes. The Rule of 72 demonstrates how different interest rates can significantly impact the growth of investments over time, emphasizing the importance of investing early and maximizing the potential for compound growth.

In conclusion, understanding the Rule of 72 and the power of compound interest can guide your financial decisions and motivate you to start saving and investing early. Small contributions made consistently over time can lead to substantial wealth in the future, providing financial security and helping you achieve your long-term goals.

Use the Magic Wisely

Now that you know the secret of the Rule of 72, you can use it to plan your financial adventures. Whether you're saving for a magical toy, a magical pet, or even a magical castle, understanding how long it takes for your money to double can help you make smart decisions.

Remember, the Rule of 72 is a powerful tool, but it's like a map. It gives you a general idea of where you're going, but the real journey depends on how you use your money and make decisions.

Double Trouble in 72!

In India, there was a wise and fair raja. He told his people to give most of their rice to him, promising to keep it safe for tough times so nobody would go hungry. At first, people gave him rice, and everything was fine. But then a year with bad rice came, and there was hunger. The people had no rice for themselves or the raja. His helpers asked him to share the rice, but he said no. They worried about how long the hunger would last.

Time passed, and people got hungrier, but the raja didn't share the rice. One day, he had a big feast. A girl named Rani saw rice falling from a basket an elephant carried. She collected it, and the raja asked what she wanted. She asked for one grain of rice today, then double that tomorrow, and double it every day. He agreed, and she got her one grain of rice.

The next day, she got two grains, then four, and so on. Rani ended up with more than a billion grains of rice. She wanted to give it to the hungry and some for the raja, but only if he promised to take what he needed. The raja agreed, and he became wise and fair. Now, think about this with money. Would you rather have a million dollars or a penny that doubles each day for a month?

After reading the story, the choice is clear. Having a single penny that doubles every day for a month is better than $1 million upfront. This is because of something called compound interest. If you took a penny and doubled it every day, by day 30, you'd have over $5 million.

The Hidden Cost of Interest

Imagine walking into a store to buy your favorite candy bar, a new pair of shoes, or even the latest smartphone. You're excited about your purchase, but there's something you might not realize, you could end up paying double or more for that item over time. Welcome to the world of interest, where the price you see on the tag isn't necessarily what you'll ultimately pay.

From everyday items like candy bars to more substantial investments like cars and houses, interest has a way of sneaking into your expenses and inflating the final cost. If you've ever wondered why your financial health matters when buying a simple candy bar or making significant purchases like a car or a house, this chapter will provide you with the insights you need to navigate the world of interest and keep your hard-earned money where it belongs. In your pocket!

Interest is a financial concept that's split into two sides: earning and paying. Let's break it down and see how it impacts your FUN Score. To start off, earned interest is the money you make from your investments over a certain time. It's like your reward for letting your money work for you.

Accrued interest is the interest that accumulates on your investments over time but has not yet been received or paid out. Think of it as money that's on its way to you, accruing value but not yet in your pocket. For example, if you own a bond, it accrues interest daily, but you may only receive the interest payments semi-annually. This means that even though the interest is building up, you won't actually see it until the payment date arrives.

Paid interest, on the other hand, refers to the interest that has already been received or paid. If you have a savings account, the interest you see credited to your account periodically is paid interest. This is the actual cash you've received from your investment returns. Similarly, if you've borrowed money, the interest payments you've made on that loan are also considered paid interest. It's the cost you've already incurred for the privilege of borrowing money.

Understanding the difference between accrued and paid interest is crucial for effective financial management. It's like knowing the flavors of ice cream at a parlor, choosing the right one can significantly enhance your experience. For instance, recognizing accrued interest on your investments can help you better forecast your income and plan for future expenses. Conversely, being aware of the interest you've already paid can aid in budgeting and managing your cash flow.

Here's the bottom line, understanding these different types of interest can give you a significant advantage in managing your finances and making informed investment decisions. It's like having an insider's guide to the financial world. With this knowledge, you can strategically plan your investments, optimize your returns, and ensure that you are not caught off guard by unexpected interest payments. In essence, getting a grip on accrued and paid interest helps you navigate the complexities of finance with confidence and ease, making your financial journey much smoother and more rewarding.

Building Bonds Beyond Transactions

In our society, a harsh reality exists, a significant number of older individuals grapple with isolation and solitude. This is particularly true among retirees who often find themselves distanced from family, devoid of the camaraderie of coworkers, and missing the daily interactions that once filled their lives. The absence of these social connections can lead to feelings of loneliness and depression, highlighting the profound need for companionship in their lives.

Companionship is a fundamental human need that significantly impacts emotional and physical well-being. Studies have shown that regular social interaction can reduce stress, improve mental health, and even extend lifespan. This need for connection is where the role of customers and routine business interactions becomes incredibly important.

Remarkably, some of the closest relationships we form in life are with cherished regular customers and those we engage with through routine business interactions. For example, think of a retiree who visits the same coffee shop every morning. Over time, they form a bond with the barista who knows their name, their favorite drink, and asks about their day. These small, consistent interactions build a sense of familiarity and belonging.

In another instance, consider an elderly person who frequents the local grocery store. The staff's friendly greetings and assistance can make them feel valued and remembered, creating a supportive community environment. These daily or weekly encounters provide structure and a sense of continuity, which are especially important as other aspects of their social life may dwindle.

The consistent service provided by businesses and their employees forges a profound connection with customers, often transcending time and keeping relationships strong even as years and decades pass. This mutual service creates a sense of loyalty and friendship that can become a cornerstone of the older individual's social life.

It's a testament to the remarkable bonding power of mutual service and the importance of fostering these connections. By recognizing and valuing the relationships formed through everyday interactions, businesses and individuals can play a crucial role in combating isolation and promoting a sense of community and belonging among older adults.

However, this notion extends beyond personal relationships; it's a principle that holds true in various aspects of life and business. Just as serving customers can create lasting connections, businesses can thrive when they invest in nurturing relationships with their clients. This investment goes beyond the transactions themselves, building trust and loyalty that can withstand challenges and changes.

Similarly, when considering investing in your grandchildren's future, the approach is not limited to simply handing over cash. Much like the enduring relationships formed through consistent service, investing in their future can create lasting impacts. This thoughtful approach combines financial wisdom with a personal touch, echoing the same principles that foster close bonds with valued customers.

But just as not all business strategies suit every client, not all investment options fit every financial scenario. The same principle applies to grandparenting. Exploring various investment avenues tailored to your specific situation is essential. It's an exercise that calls for careful evaluation, strategic thinking, and a dash of empathy that resonates both in life and business.

Ultimately, the parallels are striking. Just as serving customers leads to cherished relationships, investment choices for grandchildren can lead to lasting financial legacies. It's about understanding needs, making informed decisions, and investing in a future that reflects the values and priorities shared in both life and business. Setting up a Roth IRA for your grandchildren can be an excellent way to provide them with a head start on their financial journey. Since withdrawals from Individual Retirement Accounts are tax-free, your grandchildren can have more flexibility in using the funds when they need them. This investment can help secure their financial wellbeing, especially during retirement.

If you want to support your grandchildren's educational expenses, a Coverdell Education Savings Account is a tax-free option. By contributing to this account, you can help ease the financial burden of education costs and give them the gift of knowledge and learning. A 529 Savings Plan is another valuable option for funding your grandchildren's education. With two types available, prepaid tuition plans and college savings plans, you can choose the one that best aligns with your family's educational goals. Keep in mind that these plans may impact the amount of financial aid your grandchildren receive, so it's essential to consider the financial situation of everyone involved in the educational expenses. Trusts, if you're considering a substantial investment of $25,000 or more, setting up a trust can be a wise decision. Trusts offer greater control and flexibility over the funds, allowing you to tailor the investment strategy to suit your grandchildren's needs.

For smaller gifts, UGMA or UTMA custodial accounts can be an excellent choice. These accounts enable you to transfer assets to a minor and can be used for any purpose, not limited to educational expenses. They offer a simple and effective way to support your grandchildren financially.

Gifting stocks or bonds can be a valuable investment for your grandchildren's future. However, keep in mind that there may be gift tax implications if the amount exceeds $14,000 (or $28,000 jointly with your partner). Nevertheless, this type of investment can foster financial literacy and introduce your grandchildren to the world of investing. As you embark on the journey of crafting your legacy, there's more to consider than just the financial aspect. Your influence can extend beyond monetary resources, touching on the sentimental and emotional as well. The question arises, how can you ensure that your intentions are carried out exactly as you envision, even when you're no longer there to oversee it all? One effective route is through a will or other legal means. These tools allow you to map out your desires explicitly, not only in terms of financial assets but also concerning treasured heirlooms and cherished memories. By taking this step, you're not merely transferring possessions; you're preserving your legacy, values, and stories for generations to come.

This practice isn't dissimilar from wise business strategies. In the corporate world, well-structured plans are vital for seamless transitions and sustained success. Just as you guide your family's future, businesses require a roadmap to ensure their continuity and growth.

But even with a clear roadmap, making the right investment choices is paramount. This is where a qualified financial professional becomes an indispensable ally. Their expertise can align your aspirations with investment options that mirror your financial standing, interests, and goals for your grandchildren's future. Just as a business seeks the advice of industry experts, your legacy benefits from the guidance of seasoned professionals.

The investment options themselves are a varied landscape, akin to the myriad opportunities a business must navigate to thrive. But, as with a well-calculated business strategy, these investment options are tailored to create a lasting impact. With careful consideration, you have the ability to shape your grandchildren's lives in meaningful ways. In essence, legacy planning is about more than wealth distribution; it's about preserving your narrative and providing a foundation for the next chapter. It's a process that echoes the principles of business planning strategy, foresight, and thoughtful execution. In the intricate tapestry of life, the role of grandparents stands as a beacon of wisdom, care, and support. Just as the sun's rays nurture the earth, grandparents provide the nurturing sustenance required for the flourishing of their grandchildren's financial success. It's a remarkable journey that not only shapes the lives of young minds but also holds insights that echo in the realm of business.

In this modern age, grandparents hold a pivotal role in shaping their grandchildren's financial wellbeing. From providing financial aid to sowing seeds of money management skills, their impact is profound. Much like a skilled entrepreneur nurturing a startup, grandparents set the stage for a successful financial future. Yet, like any venture, balance is key. Just as a business owner must balance investment and expenditure, grandparents must delicately navigate the fine line between lending a helping hand and maintaining their own financial stability. This act requires thoughtful consideration, aligning generosity with a sustainable plan.

Statistics reveal a heartwarming truth, Grandparents are a wellspring of support, with 9 out of 10 extending financial assistance annually. It's a testament to the love and dedication that flow through generations. But what form does this aid take? Much like diverse business strategies, grandparents offer assistance through various channels, with gifts reigning as the most common contribution.

While the magnitude of financial resources may vary, the value lies not in the quantity but in the intention. Grandparents, much like entrepreneurs, tailor their actions to their unique circumstances, values, and aspirations. Their support, whether through a surplus or within a tighter budget, is an investment that yields immeasurable returns. So, as you journey through the realm of grandparenthood, recognize the profound influence you wield. Your role extends beyond simply offering monetary aid; you're nurturing financial growth, imparting life lessons, and sowing the seeds of financial empowerment. Just as you guide your grandchildren, businesses thrive under the guidance of adept leaders. In conclusion, the path of financial empowerment for your grandchildren mirrors the journey of nurturing a prosperous business. The principles of balance, individualized strategies, and intentionality echo throughout. By treading this path thoughtfully, you shape the future, ensuring financial security, growth, and wisdom for the generations yet to come.

In the grand symphony of life, the role of grandparents emerges as a tender melody of purposeful giving. Like artisans crafting a masterpiece, grandparents direct their support towards essential areas, harmonizing education, training, and financial protection. This symphony of care echoes through generations, resonating in the realms of both family and business.

Education, the cornerstone of growth, takes center stage in this melody. With the precision of a conductor leading an orchestra, grandparents channel their resources towards funding their grandchild's education. Whether it's contributing to a college tuition fund, nurturing an education savings plan, or providing the means for educational supplies and enriching programs, every note of support contributes to the crescendo of knowledge and opportunity.

Yet, it's not solely grand gestures that define this symphony. Like delicate notes in a sonnet, seemingly small gestures hold profound meaning. A birthday gift, or a shared ice cream cone. These seemingly modest acts are threads woven with intention. It's the heart behind the gesture that transforms these moments into memories, just as a single instrument can bring depth to a musical composition. Purposeful giving transcends material offerings; it's a legacy of values, a gift that resounds through time. Much like a business anchored in its core principles, purposeful giving encapsulates intentions that stretch far beyond the present moment. It instills values of generosity, compassion, and thoughtful planning that enrich both the recipient and the giver. In the grand tapestry of life and business, purposeful giving remains a thread that binds generations together. It's a legacy that goes beyond financial contributions, extending into the realms of character, values, and shared aspirations. So, as you consider your role as a grandparent, remember that each act of purposeful giving weaves into the intricate fabric of your grandchild's life, leaving a legacy that echoes far into the future.

Grandparents can often provide financial support for various needs and life events, including:

- Birthday or holiday gifts, showing love and appreciation through thoughtful gifts.
- Day-to-day expenses, assisting with regular living costs to alleviate financial burdens.
- Vacation costs, making family experiences more accessible through financial help.
- Life events (wedding, etc.), supporting important milestones in a grandchild's life.
- Mortgage or rent, providing assistance with housing expenses.
- Healthcare, assisting with medical bills and healthcare needs.
- Childcare, supporting parents with the costs of childcare.
- Education costs, funding educational pursuits and related expenses.

Grandparents have a unique opportunity to positively influence their grandchildren's lives through financial support and guidance.

Whether it's providing financial resources for educational aspirations, offering help during challenging times, or simply sharing the joy of gift-giving, grandparents play a vital role in shaping the financial future of their loved ones. As grandparents navigate these financial decisions, it is essential to prioritize open communication and collaboration with the entire family to ensure that the support aligns with everyone's needs and aspirations.

The faster you reach your FUN Goal for financial freedom, the more time you'll have to have fun with your favorite people. Remember, time is limited, so don't forget that you have a limited amount of it to make the most of!

CHAPTER EIGHT

Achieving Financial Freedom & Investing

To succeed in the business of life, you must fall in love with it just as deeply as you would with another person. Adoration is the key! See only love, hear only love, speak only love, and feel love with all your heart. Embrace the ultimate power of love and let it infuse every aspect of your journey. Throughout your day, search for the things you love. Marvel at the technology and inventions that inspire you. Find beauty in buildings, cars, cafes, and stores. Cherish the qualities you love in others and revel in the wonders of nature, from birds and trees to flowers and scents. Your senses become conduits for love as you see, hear, smell, taste, and touch everything you adore.

Express your love openly and unreservedly. Share your admiration for your home, family, friends, and even strangers. Let them know what you love about them and watch the love flow back to you. Remind yourself daily of the things you love by making a written list, adding new items regularly. Whenever you need a lift or want to amplify your good feelings, take a moment to mentally recount everything you love and adore. Embrace simplicity in this practice and let it have an astonishing effect on your life. Your mission is to love as much as possible each day. Focus on what you love and turn away from what you don't. By doing so, your tomorrows will overflow with boundless happiness, granting you the unlimited abundance and joy you desire.

Embrace and cherish all the beauty life offers. Fall in love with every detail, from the smallest moments to the grandest experiences, and your existence will blossom into an exquisite tapestry of love and fulfillment. When you allow love to be your guiding force, it permeates every aspect of your life, transforming the mundane into the extraordinary.

Imagine waking up each day with a sense of gratitude and wonder for the world around you. Appreciating the warmth of the morning sun, the sound of birds singing, or the simple pleasure of a hot cup of coffee. These seemingly small details can bring immense joy when viewed through the lens of love and appreciation.

In your relationships, letting love guide your actions means showing kindness, patience, and understanding. It involves truly listening to others, valuing their perspectives, and nurturing connections with genuine care. This approach fosters deeper bonds and creates a supportive network that enriches your life.

Applying this mindset to your career or personal projects can also lead to remarkable outcomes. When you are passionate about what you do and approach your work with love and dedication, it reflects in the quality of your efforts. This passion can inspire others, attract opportunities, and lead to a fulfilling and successful career.

For instance, an artist who pours love into every brushstroke creates masterpieces that resonate with viewers. A teacher who genuinely cares about their students' success makes a lasting impact on their lives. A business owner who prioritizes customer satisfaction and employee well-being builds a loyal and motivated team.

Moreover, love as a guiding force helps you navigate challenges with resilience and optimism. It encourages you to see obstacles as opportunities for growth and to face adversity with courage and grace. This perspective not only enhances your problem-solving abilities but also ensures that you remain grounded and focused on what truly matters.

In essence, by embracing and falling in love with every detail of life, you create a vibrant and fulfilling existence. This love radiates outward, influencing your relationships, work, and overall well-being. Success and contentment become natural byproducts of a life lived with love at its core, leading to a rich and meaningful journey.

Active and Passive Income

Each of us has the potential to run a personal business with two essential departments, labeled active and passive income. Understanding and leveraging the differences between these two types of income can pave the way for financial success and stability.

Active income is the money earned from direct involvement in work or services. This includes salaries, hourly wages, freelance work, and any other form of compensation where you exchange time and effort for payment. For instance, a doctor earning a salary from a hospital, a graphic designer charging clients per project, or a store manager receiving a monthly paycheck all generate active income. The defining characteristic of active income is that it requires ongoing effort to maintain; if you stop working, the income stops too.

Passive income, on the other hand, is earned with little to no ongoing effort. This income stream is generated from investments, rental properties, royalties, or any other ventures where you do the work upfront and then continue to earn money over time. For example, owning a rental property and collecting monthly rent, investing in dividend-paying stocks, or receiving royalties from a book or a song you created are all sources of passive income. Once the initial work is done, these income streams require minimal maintenance.

Leveraging Active and Passive Income

To achieve financial success, it's crucial to balance and integrate both active and passive income streams. Here's how to leverage them effectively:

1. Active Income as a Foundation: Active income provides the immediate funds necessary for day-to-day living expenses and initial investments. It forms the financial base upon which you can build. For instance, while working a full-time job (active income), you can save a portion of your salary to invest in passive income opportunities.
2. Transitioning to Passive Income: Once you have a stable source of active income, the next step is to invest in assets that generate passive income. This could mean buying rental properties, investing in stocks or bonds, starting a side business that can eventually run without your constant involvement, or creating digital products like e-books or online courses. The goal is to create multiple streams of income that don't require your active participation.
3. Benefits of Passive Income: Passive income provides financial security and freedom. It allows you to earn money while focusing on other pursuits, such as spending time with family, traveling, or even starting new business ventures. For example, a person with rental income from several properties can potentially retire early or reduce their working hours, knowing they have a steady income stream.
4. Diversification and Risk Management: Combining active and passive income streams also helps diversify your income sources, reducing financial risk. If you rely solely on active income, a job loss or illness could severely impact your finances. However, with passive income in place, you have a financial cushion that provides stability during uncertain times.

Examples

- Active Income Example: A software engineer earns $120,000 a year working for a tech company. This income is dependent on their continuous employment and performance.
- Passive Income Example: The same software engineer invests in real estate and earns $20,000 annually from rental properties. They also invest in dividend-paying stocks that generate an additional $5,000 per year.

By understanding and strategically combining active and passive income, you can create a robust financial portfolio. This approach not only enhances your earning potential but also ensures long-term financial health and independence.

Active income requires direct participation in work-related activities to earn money. This includes traditional sources such as wages, salaries, tips, commissions, freelance income, side hustles, and any other income that comes from actively trading your time for compensation. On the other hand, passive income comes from owning income-producing assets. It involves earning money without actively participating in work-related activities. Passive income sources can range from investments, dividends, and real estate rentals to business ownership, online businesses, courses, downloadable content, YouTube channels, website display ads, and affiliate marketing.

The true power lies in combining both active and passive income streams to enhance your financial situation significantly. By focusing on increasing your active income, you can save more money each month. These savings can then be strategically invested in income-generating assets like investments, businesses, rental real estate, or high-interest accounts. This creates a positive feedback loop where your active income fuels your ability to invest in passive income sources.

As you continue to invest in passive income, your annual earnings have the potential to grow substantially. Eventually, the returns from your passive income sources may even surpass your active income, leading you to achieve financial independence. At this stage, you can sustain your lifestyle solely through passive income, giving you the freedom to choose how you spend your time without being tied to traditional work.

Embracing and optimizing both active and passive income streams can be the key to financial success and security. It allows you to build wealth, generate multiple income streams, and ultimately attain the desired financial independence that provides a comfortable and fulfilling life.

Active income and passive income are taxed differently by the IRS. Active income is typically taxed at your regular income tax rates, while passive income may have different tax rates depending on how it is earned. Working with a tax professional is recommended for managing taxes on passive income streams.

Combining active and passive income can be a powerful way to increase overall earnings. By focusing on increasing active income and saving a portion of it, you can invest in income-generating assets, which will compound over time and increase your passive income. The goal is to eventually achieve financial independence, where your passive income covers your living expenses.

Starting with active income and gradually transitioning to passive income over time is a common path towards financial independence and retirement. Investing in income-producing assets today is crucial for building a comfortable retirement and securing a long-term financial strategy. Both active and passive income play important roles in this journey towards financial freedom.

Combining Active and Passive Income for Increased Earnings

Let's explore how combining active and passive income can lead to a substantial increase in overall earnings. Suppose you have an hourly rate of $20, and your annual income amounts to $41,600 based on this rate. To boost your financial prospects, you decide to invest 15% of your income, which comes to $6,240 per year.

Over the next five years, assuming your investments yield an average return of 8% annually, your investment will grow to over $45,000. Now, this $45,000 earning an 8% return will generate an additional $3,600 in the following year. Essentially, this extra income is like giving yourself a $1.73 raise, without requiring any extra work.

The key takeaway is that a combination of active income from your job and passive income from investments can significantly enhance your financial situation. By saving and investing a portion of your active income, you can create a source of passive income that compounds over time, ultimately leading to greater financial stability.

Both active and passive income play vital roles in achieving financial independence and eventually, retirement. You typically begin your journey with active income, working for a company or running your own business. As you accumulate savings and invest wisely, you can gradually transition to earning more from passive income streams.

The ultimate goal is to reach a point where your passive income covers all your living expenses, allowing you to retire comfortably without relying on active work. To accomplish this, it's essential to start investing in income-producing assets today. This long-term strategy lays the foundation for a secure and comfortable retirement in the future.

Opportunities and Blessings

In the world of business, love is being alert to the opportunities and blessings that surround you. To truly thrive, you must be keenly aware of everything unfolding around you, or else you risk missing out on valuable prospects.

Stay attentive to the things that you love, whether it's a brilliant business idea, a potential partnership, or the admiration of your clients. Listen intently to the feedback and needs of your customers, as they hold the key to your success. Pay attention to the industry trends, market shifts, and innovations that could shape your business landscape.

Just like being alert on the streets, your business senses must be finely tuned to catch the subtle signs and signals that might otherwise pass you by. Avoid being hypnotized by the incessant chatter of your thoughts and the noise of distractions. Instead, train yourself to focus on the present moment, embracing the fullness of each experience.

Have you ever had a breakthrough moment when a great idea came to you seemingly out of nowhere? That's the power of heightened awareness. By immersing yourself in the love of your work and your industry, you elevate your level of alertness and creativity. In business, staying alert brings the advantage of swift decision-making, nimble adaptability, and the ability to seize opportunities when they arise. Just as calling out a friend's name can awaken them from a trance, love has the power to keep you wide awake to the endless possibilities that surround you.

So, cultivate a habit of conscious observation and appreciation. Notice the little details that others may overlook, for therein lie hidden treasures. Love your business, your team, your customers, and everything that contributes to your growth. As you infuse your endeavors with love and attentiveness, you'll unlock the key to a thriving and prosperous business journey.

Gratitude is the Key

In both life and business, gratitude is the powerful key that unlocks abundance and attracts more of the things we cherish. When we embrace gratitude, even for the smallest blessings, we open the floodgates for greater prosperity in all aspects of our journey. Start with two simple words "thank you" and let them flow from the depths of your heart. When you express gratitude genuinely and wholeheartedly, you infuse your life and business with love. This love is the fuel that ignites the great multiplier of life.

Gratitude for what you have. Embrace gratitude for every little thing you possess, no matter how seemingly insignificant. Be grateful for the money you have, regardless of its amount. The more you appreciate your financial resources, the more you will attract prosperity into your life. Express gratitude for the relationships you have, recognizing their value and potential for growth. Through gratitude, even imperfect relationships can blossom and evolve positively. Be grateful for the job you currently have, even if it falls short of your dreams. Your gratitude will open doors to better opportunities in your career.

Cultivate a mindset of perpetual gratitude. Let "thank you" become a natural part of your vocabulary and inner dialogue. As you immerse yourself in this state of gratitude, you will experience an ever-deepening sense of appreciation and love for the world around you. This love is a magnet for more abundance and fulfillment in both your personal and professional endeavors. Gratitude is not just about receiving; it is a powerful way to give love. When you express gratitude to others for their contributions, kindness, and support, you uplift their spirits and strengthen your connections. In business, showing appreciation to your team, customers, and partners fosters a positive and harmonious work environment. In life, sharing gratitude with loved ones enhances your bonds and brings joy to everyone involved.

As you embrace gratitude as a way of life and a force of giving love, you'll experience the transformative effects it has on every aspect of your journey. Gratitude becomes the catalyst that multiplies your blessings, amplifies your successes, and fills your life and business with abundance beyond measure. So, from the simplest pleasures to the grandest achievements, let gratitude be your guiding light, and watch as the world unfolds with newfound richness and fulfillment.

Take a moment to reflect honestly on your feelings about money. Do you truly love money, or does its absence cause you to feel uneasy? If you have all the money you need, then certainly you feel positive about it. However, if you find yourself lacking in financial resources, it might indicate that your feelings towards money are not entirely positive.

Changing the way you feel about money can have a profound impact on the financial abundance in your life. When you cultivate positive feelings towards money, you attract more of it towards you. If you find yourself in a position where you don't have much money and receive bills, it might not make you feel good. However, reacting negatively to these bills only perpetuates the cycle of financial strain. What you give out, you receive back.

Perspective (Bills)

To break this pattern, it's essential to approach paying bills with a different perspective. Use your imagination to transform bills into something that brings you joy. Instead of seeing them as burdens, envision them as opportunities to give back and appreciate the services you've received. Imagine that you're graciously donating money out of the goodness of your heart, acknowledging the value provided by each company or person. Turn your bills into checks you're receiving or an expression of gratitude for the services rendered.

Even if you don't have immediate funds to pay a bill, express your gratitude and visualize the money flowing in to cover the expenses. The law of attraction doesn't differentiate between reality and imagination; it responds to the feelings you emit. When you receive your salary, embrace gratitude wholeheartedly. Rather than worrying about making it last, use this moment as an opportunity to give love. Being grateful for your income will attract more financial blessings into your life. Don't dismiss even the smallest amounts; be thankful for every bit that comes your way. Remember, what you're grateful for will multiply. Gratitude is a powerful multiplier.

Changing the way you feel about money and adopting a positive and appreciative outlook will transform your financial reality. Embrace the art of gratitude and watch as abundance and prosperity effortlessly find their way into your life, empowering you to create the business of You with abundance and fulfillment.

Beliefs about Money

Observe the world around you, and you'll notice that many people harbor negative feelings about money. Surprisingly, wealthy individuals differ from the rest primarily in how they perceive money. They hold more positive beliefs and emotions towards it, and that's the key. So, why do so many people feel negatively about money? It isn't because they have never had it. In fact, many wealthy individuals started with very little. The root cause lies in the negative beliefs about money ingrained in their minds during childhood. Statements like "We can't afford that," "Money is evil," or "Rich people are dishonest" unknowingly shape their feelings towards money.

As children, we tend to accept and internalize what our parents, teachers, or society tell us, leading to the development of negative money beliefs. We might have been taught that wanting money is wrong or unspiritual and that having ample money requires exhausting hard work. But here's the revelation: none of these beliefs are true. The people who shared these ideas did so innocently, based on their own beliefs. However, the law of attraction works differently. If you find yourself lacking money, it is likely because you are emitting more negative feelings about money than positive ones.

Now, it's time to challenge and transform these limiting beliefs. Understand that it's possible to love money and maintain spiritual integrity. Money is not evil; it is a tool that can create positive change and opportunities. You have the power to change your beliefs and feelings towards money. Remember, life operates on a different principle. When you give out genuine love and positive feelings about money, the law of attraction responds in kind, bringing more prosperity and financial well-being into your experience. So, examine your relationship with money, release negative beliefs, and open yourself to a new reality of abundance and financial freedom.

Play with Money

Seizing every opportunity to play with money can transform your financial reality and business endeavors. Embrace the mindset of abundance and joy each time you handle money, for it holds the key to multiplying your wealth. Feel love and gratitude as you pay for anything or hand over money. Imagine how your money is contributing to the success of the company and supporting its staff. By feeling good about the money you're giving, you shift from scarcity to abundance, paving the way for financial prosperity.

To make this practice more fun and effective, play a game with yourself. Visualize each dollar bill as a symbol of abundance. The front of the dollar bill represents plenty of money, while the back symbolizes a lack of money. Whenever you handle money, consciously orient the bills so that the front side is facing you. Arrange your bills in your wallet with the front side showing, and when you hand over money, ensure the front side is upward. Even when using a credit card, imagine it as a symbol of abundance with your name on it. Playfully "Rip" the credit card to the front where your name is, reinforcing the idea that you have unlimited financial opportunities.

By engaging in this playful ritual, you reinforce positive feelings about money and invite more abundance into your life and business. Embrace each money moment with love and gratitude, knowing that your positive energy attracts more wealth and financial success. Seize the opportunity to play with money and watch as the business of You flourishes with boundless prosperity and fulfillment.

In the realm of career and business, it's the irresistible force of love that propels the flow of money. Those who exude love by feeling good become magnetic to wealth and abundance. Remember, you don't need to prove your worth by constantly striving to earn money; you are already deserving of all the financial abundance you require, here and now! Your true purpose is to work joyfully, driven by passion and excitement for what you do. Love your work, and money will naturally follow!

If you find yourself in a job solely for the sake of earning money, without genuine love for it, you won't attract the job you truly desire.

Instead, focus on the job you love, which already exists in the present moment. To manifest this ideal job, immerse yourself in the feeling of already having it. Embrace and cherish the positive aspects of your current job because when you offer love and appreciation, everything you love will come to you. Your dream job will effortlessly walk into your life!

Even during times when your business may experience a slight dip, reacting with negative feelings can amplify the downturn. To unleash the creative inspirations and ideas that will skyrocket your business to unimaginable heights, tune in to the frequency of love. Find ways to uplift your spirits and feel good about your business. Play, imagine, and create games that elevate your emotions, for when you lift your feelings, your business will soar.

In every facet of life, each day, shower love on everything you see, everything around you, and celebrate the success of other companies as if it were your own. Embrace a genuine sense of happiness for others' accomplishments, and you will attract success to yourself. In business or any job, ensure that you provide equal value in return for the money you receive, and even more if possible. Giving more value than what you receive ensures the success of your business or career.

Remember, the law of attraction responds to the love and positive energy you emanate. Infuse your career and business with love, passion, and gratitude, and watch as your path becomes paved with prosperity and fulfillment. The business of You thrives when fueled by the boundless force of love. In life and business, money serves as a tool to bring you closer to the things you truly love and cherish. Instead of solely fixating on money, shift your focus to the delightful experiences and possibilities it can offer. Envision yourself surrounded by the people and activities you love, relishing the joy they bring. Embrace the things you love and the feelings they evoke, for that is where you will find true fulfillment.

The irresistible force of love presents numerous avenues to manifest your desires, and money is just one of them. By tapping into the boundless power of love, you open yourself to infinite possibilities and attract what you seek through various channels, not solely dependent on financial means. Embrace love as your guiding force and watch as life and business unfold in extraordinary ways beyond your wildest dreams. In the realm of business, the fundamental rule remains unchanged; love must always take precedence over money. Placing love as the guiding force in your endeavors is crucial, for any deviation from this principle will incur the consequences of love's law of attraction. Love should reign supreme, and nothing should supersede it, not even money.

Money serves as a valuable tool, drawn into your life through the power of love. However, it is essential to avoid prioritizing money over love. If money becomes the dominant focus, it can lead to an influx of negative outcomes in various aspects of your business and life. Neglecting love in your interactions with others can open the door to negativity, impacting relationships, well-being, happiness, and financial prosperity. You are destined to experience abundance and sufficiency in your business endeavors. Scarcity is not your true path, as it contributes to negativity in the world. Embrace the beauty of life by placing love at the forefront and watch as the money you need to lead a fulfilling existence effortlessly flows into your business and your life. Love, the ultimate guiding force, is the key to unlocking the fullness of life's potential in the realm of business and beyond. Remember, what you give to others is the foundation of your own reality. Embrace the transformative power of love, kindness, and empathy in your partnership and parenting journey, and watch as a life of fulfillment and joy unfolds.

The Business Inside Your Body: Unlocking Financial Freedom

So, here's the deal, your body is like a bustling marketplace, with all sorts of transactions taking place every single second. Think about your heart pumping blood, your lungs breathing in air, and your cells converting food into energy. It's like a high-speed exchange of goods and services, but on a microscopic level. Let's connect the dots between this invisible business and financial freedom. Just like in the corporate world, your body's "business" requires resources to keep running smoothly. Imagine your cells as diligent employees, working non-stop to keep the company or your body up and running. But here's the twist, you're the CEO, calling the shots and making strategic decisions. Every choice you make, from what you eat to how you move, impacts this internal business. The quality of "inputs" like nutritious meals and regular exercise directly affects the "outputs," which could be your overall health, energy levels, and even your mood.

So, think about it this way. You're not just a passive participant in this business venture. You're the CEO, the decision-maker, and the beneficiary. Your health is the capital, and every healthy choice you make is an investment that pays dividends in the form of a vibrant life and financial freedom.

In the next chapters, we'll dive into practical strategies to optimize this "Business Inside Your Body." From smart nutrition choices to staying active, we'll uncover the secret to not only feeling fantastic but also paving the way to financial freedom. So, buckle up, we're about to take your journey to a whole new level!

Investing Beyond the Dollars

Let's take a moment and explore what investing truly means to us. Close your eyes and think about it. What springs to mind when someone drops the "investing" bomb? Is it a whirlwind of insurance policies, mutual funds, stock market frenzy, or perhaps visions of high-yield investments dancing in your head? Maybe for some, it's the thought of safeguarding a nest egg for the next generation, or an uncomfortable feeling that investing is as complex as quantum physics. And yes, there are folks out there who only entertain the idea of investing when their time in this world starts to tick like a time bomb. But here's a curveball. Did you know that many of us are investing even when we don't realize it? Yes, siree! Think about those gym memberships, personal trainers, health supplements, and beauty treatments that gobble up a fair share of our budgets. We're investing in our health, our well-being, and even our vanity! Ever wonder about the massive ad budgets of beauty companies, all vying to make you feel younger, healthier, and more fabulous? That's an investment too, folks!

Let's spill the beans on the secret we're talking about here: the most monumental investment you can ever make in this roller coaster of life. Drum roll, please... It's the investment in yourself! Yeah, you heard me right. It's about nurturing your mind, body, and soul for the long game. Your personal development, your skills, your knowledge, that's the jackpot right there. Sure, the financial markets have their allure, and building wealth is vital. But remember, it's not just about the dollars. It's about investing in your health, your growth, and your happiness. Imagine being the CEO of "You Inc." making decisions that boost your well-being, enhance your skills, and create a foundation for success. So, next time you hear the word "investing," let it remind you that you're not just parking money in accounts; you're also putting time, energy, and resources into crafting the best version of yourself. It's the ultimate power move, and guess what? You're the chief beneficiary. So, let's dive into the nitty-gritty of what this self-investment entails, because the journey to financial IQ starts with nurturing the most valuable asset you have.

The Ultimate Investment: YOU

Alright, folks, let's talk about the golden rule of all rules, the one that'll take you places you've never even dreamed of, "Invest in Yourself." Sounds simple, right? Well, it is, and it's the kind of simple that's secretly super powerful. Let's start with a reality check. Your parents, bless their hearts, will give you the education ticket, but it's a one-way trip that drops you off at adulthood station. Education is like an appetizer, but it won't satisfy your hunger for financial smarts. That's where self-investment swoops in like a financial superhero. So, imagine this: you're the captain of your own ship, steering toward the land of financial freedom. And guess what? The ship is YOU. Yep, you're the vessel that carries you through life's storms and calms. But here's the kicker, if you don't invest in yourself, who will? It's like having the most incredible business idea but never putting a dime into it.

Let's debunk a myth while we're at it. Those fancy college degrees and diplomas? They're golden, sure, but they're like training wheels on a bike. They give you a foundation, but they don't teach you how to ride the journey of making money. Colleges might teach you skills to work for others, but what about building your own empire?

And business school? Don't get us wrong, they're great, but if these business wizards were that successful, wouldn't they be out there conquering the business world instead of teaching about it? And your boss? Don't count on them handing over the keys to success. They've got their own kingdom to build. The truth is, you're the mastermind behind your success. You're the CEO of your life's venture and investing in yourself is like buying stock in the best company out there; You Enterprises. Whether it's learning new skills, gaining knowledge, or refining your talents, these investments pay the best dividends.

So, here's the plan, educate yourself, soak in knowledge, learn from the best, and grow like a champ. Invest time, effort, and yes, even money, into expanding your skill set. It's not just about getting by; it's about thriving. Remember, the ultimate jackpot is YOU. So, go on, take a leap, and invest in the greatest venture of all your future, your growth, and your success. Because, at the end of the day, you're the only one who can bet big on the unstoppable force that is YOU.

CHAPTER NINE

Providing Value and Growing Your Income

When it comes to whether salary or hourly work is favored by lenders, there isn't a one-size-fits-all answer. Lenders evaluate various aspects of your financial situation to determine your eligibility for financing and the terms they can offer. Both salary and hourly work have their own considerations.

Salary

- Pros: A consistent salary is often viewed positively by lenders because it represents stable and predictable income. It indicates a regular flow of money, which can be reassuring for lenders assessing your ability to repay loans.
- Cons: A higher salary might not necessarily guarantee better financing terms if you have significant existing debts or other financial responsibilities. Lenders also consider your debt-to-income ratio, which compares your monthly debt payments to your income.

Hourly Work

- Pros: Hourly work can be beneficial if your hours are stable and predictable. Lenders may also consider your work history, the industry you're in, and the likelihood of continued employment.

- Cons: If your hourly work hours are irregular or fluctuating, lenders might view your income as less stable, potentially affecting your financing terms.

Lenders often favor consistent income, whether it's from a salary or hourly work. Having a reliable employment history and a track record of steady income can be favorable. Assess your ability to manage additional debt based on your debt-to-income ratio. Regardless of whether you're salaried or hourly, a high debt-to-income ratio can impact your financing terms. The stability of the industry you work in and the demand for your occupation also play a role. Certain industries or occupations may have more favorable perceptions in lending assessments.

Lenders aim to gauge your ability to repay loans based on your overall financial situation. Providing accurate and complete information about your income, whether salary or hourly, is essential for transparent and fair lending evaluations. Understanding that lenders assess your income based on its stability and consistency, rather than the specific type (salary or hourly), empowers you to present your financial situation in the best light. Whether you're salaried or hourly, highlighting your employment history, consistent income, and responsible financial management can positively influence your financing terms.

By focusing on maintaining a stable income, managing debts responsibly, and showcasing your financial stability, you can position yourself favorably in the eyes of lenders. This understanding enables you to strategically manage your finances and approach financing opportunities with confidence, paving the way for better terms that align with your goals.

Getting Rich by Providing Value

Getting rich quickly might sound appealing, but the real path to wealth lies in a simple yet powerful strategy; providing value in your job. Whether you're just starting your career or looking to enhance your financial prospects, this approach can set you on the path to financial success. Let's break it down into easy steps and explore how this concept can elevate your life and financial journey.

View Your Job as an Opportunity

Focus on increasing your W2 income by providing more value. Your job isn't just a way to pay the bills; it's an opportunity to build wealth. How? Consider the potential of real estate. Buying and holding properties as rentals is a proven way to grow wealth over time. The catch? Qualifying for real estate investments often requires a solid income history. That's where your job comes in. Your W2 income, the income reported on your tax form from your job, can be a ticket to real estate investments. To increase your ability to qualify for loans, concentrate on boosting your W2 income.

Provide More Value

Here's the key! The more value you bring to your workplace, the more you'll be compensated. Imagine you work in an office. Can you become more efficient? If you learn another language, can that benefit your company's operations? Think about ways to solve bigger problems or contribute to the business's growth. The more valuable you are to your employer, the more you can potentially earn.

In the pursuit of wealth, remember this essential lesson. Give before you expect to receive. Many people have it backwards; they expect a raise before putting in extra effort. Instead, focus on providing value first. Solve problems, work harder, and strive to make a meaningful impact. The more you give, the luckier you become, and the more you can earn. It's easy to fall into the trap of waiting for a bigger paycheck to come your way. Your proactive approach can lead to significant rewards.

Understanding the link between providing value and increasing your income empowers you. By homing in on how you can contribute more to your job, you not only open doors for career growth but also create opportunities for real estate investments. With higher W2 income, you'll be better positioned to qualify for loans, allowing you to build wealth through real estate.

This concept extends beyond finance. By focusing on providing value, you enhance your skills, boost your confidence, and build a reputation as a valuable team member. These qualities can open doors for advancement, networking, and even potential entrepreneurial pursuits. So, grab that notepad and reflect. How can you provide more value in your job? What skills can you develop, or problems can you solve? Start by giving more, and you'll discover that the path to financial prosperity and personal fulfillment is right in your hands.

Steps to Financial Freedom

1. Start with a $1,000 emergency fund. This is your safety net for unexpected expenses.
2. Pay off all your debt using the debt snowball method. It's about getting rid of financial burdens one at a time.

3. Save three to six months' worth of expenses in a fully funded emergency fund. Now you're more financially secure.
4. Invest 15% of your household income into retirement. Increase your FUN score.
5. Begin saving for your kids' college funds, so they don't have to deal with student loan debt.
6. Pay off your house early (preferably in less than 15 years), and you're on top of your financial game.
7. Reach your FUN Goal and give generously. Enjoy the fruits of your financial discipline and help others along the way.

Escape Routes from a Tight Spot

We've all been there! Stuck in a financial pickle. But fear not, because this chapter is your ultimate guide to breaking free from that mess and paving a path toward financial clarity. Let's explore the two tried-and-true methods that can lead you out of the maze.

- Method 1: Assess and Strategize. Imagine you're in the heart of a dense forest, and the first step is to take a deep breath and assess your surroundings. The same goes for your financial mess. Take a close look at your financial situation, your income, expenses, debts, and assets. It might be a tough reality check, but acknowledging where you stand is the first step to getting back on track. Now, it's time to strategize. Think of this as planning your way out of the forest. Create a budget that aligns with your financial goals. Cut down unnecessary expenses and find ways to increase your income. Prioritize paying off high-interest debts and building an emergency fund.

- Method 2: Seek Expert Guidance. Just like a traveler might ask for directions, don't hesitate to seek help when navigating a financial mess. Financial advisors, credit counselors, and experts in the field are your guides to finding the best route out of the chaos. They can offer insights, strategies, and personalized advice tailored to your situation. Remember, getting out of a financial mess takes time and effort. It's like climbing a mountain one step at a time. Stay committed to your budget, track your progress, and celebrate each milestone you reach. Over time, you'll find yourself climbing higher and closer to the peak of financial stability.

Whether you choose to assess and strategize on your own or enlist the help of financial experts, the key is to take action. The path to financial freedom might have twists and turns, but with determination and the right strategies, you can make your way out of the maze and into a brighter financial future. It's time to take the first step and pave your way to financial clarity and success.

Cash Flow Kingdom: Trim, Streamline, and Invest for Success

Alright, fellow money enthusiasts, we're diving deep into the heart of the financial game. This chapter is your golden ticket to boosting your cash flow, cutting unnecessary expenses, and setting the stage for entrepreneurial triumph. Buckle up, we're about to transform your spending habits into financial expertise.

Cash flow is the ultimate MVP as you're crafting your master plan for a business venture. Cash flow isn't just a term; it's the pulse that keeps your venture alive. It's the lifeline that fuels growth, pays the bills, and keeps you in the game. So, before you launch into entrepreneurship, it's time to clean house. Trim the fat and say goodbye to unnecessary spending by uncluttering your financial closet.

Trim the Fat

It's time to cut down on expenses that might be draining your pockets. We're talking about smoking. Maybe don't quit cold turkey, but a few less sticks can save you a lot. Alcohol? Sure, enjoy, but don't let it become a financial black hole. Night outs? Swap some for nights in, pondering how to rake in extra bucks.

Invest in Value

Would you start a marathon with weights around your ankles? Exactly. Don't kickstart your business with financial baggage. As you trim your expenses, start thinking about what you can invest in today that will pump funds into your pockets tomorrow. It's like planting seeds with the right investments can grow into substantial financial forests.

Guard Your Cash

Think of liabilities as stealthy money snatchers. They might seem harmless, but they're bleeding your finances. Anything that takes money out of your wallet without the promise of future returns is a liability. Shift your focus to assets that put money back in your pocket.

Kick Laziness to the Curb

Laziness is a sneaky saboteur. It's the champion procrastinator that loves to derail success. It's time to kick laziness to the curb and embrace a work ethic that propels you forward. Remember, your journey to success is an active one. It's about taking steps, making moves, and hustling for your financial future.

Trim those expenses, channel your resources into value-generating investments, and guard your cash flow like the treasure it is. It's about aligning your spending habits with your financial dreams and transforming every dollar into a building block of your empire. Your financial success is waiting. It's time to make cash flow your ally and set the stage for entrepreneurial victory.

Unleashing Your Offensive Arsenal: Winning Strategies for Business Skill Mastery

Alright, game-changers, we're shifting into offensive mode. This chapter is your playbook for boosting your business skills without breaking the bank. Get ready to seize the spotlight and transform your business game with savvy strategies that pack a punch.

Continuous Learning

The treasure chest of knowledge lies right at your fingertips. It's time to unlock it with continuous learning. This isn't about expensive courses or high-priced workshops. We're talking about low-cost ways to level up your skills. Dive into online tutorials, tap into podcasts, and devour books that expand your expertise.

Networking

You're only as strong as your connections. Networking is your superpower when it comes to mastering business skills. Attend local events, webinars, and seminars. These gatherings are golden opportunities to learn from experts and connect with like-minded professionals. It's like building an army of allies who are ready to share insights and experiences.

Mentorship

Imagine having a seasoned pro by your side, guiding you through the twists and turns of business. Seek out mentors who have been where you want to go. Their experience and insights are invaluable assets on your journey to skill mastery.

Practice

Just like a musician hones their craft, you need to practice your business skills to perfection. It's about taking what you've learned and putting it into action. Whether it's negotiating deals, marketing strategies, or financial analysis, practice refines your skills and turns them into second nature.

The Scoop

Offensive strategies are your ticket to mastering business skills. From continuous learning to networking, mentorship, and relentless practice, these tactics are your keys to unlocking expertise. And remember, you don't need a fortune to invest; it's about investing your time and effort in the right places.

As you dive into this chapter, think of yourself as an athlete training for the Olympics. The hard work, the sweat, and the dedication pay off when you step onto the field fully equipped with winning strategies. Your business skills are your competitive edge, and with the right playbook, you're ready to dominate the game. It's time to go on the offensive and write your own success story.

Adjust Your Priorities

Sometimes, we have to choose between what we want and what we need. It's like deciding between spending $9 on something you really like or $11 on something you like a lot. To be happy, try to spend a little less than what you make. That way, you'll have more money to put into your magic money jar!

Change Your Thinking

Our thoughts are like magic spells. If we believe we deserve good things, they are more likely to happen! Some people who win big prizes end up losing everything because they didn't think carefully about their money. But you can be different! Believe in yourself and the magic of saving, and you'll see amazing things happen!

Adjust Your Lifestyle

Imagine you have a treasure chest with precious coins. You don't want to spend all your coins on little things you only want for a short time. Instead, focus on the big treasures, like food, shelter, and water, which are the things you really need. Save your coins for things that will make your dreams come true!

Earn Additional Income

Just like having a lemonade stand or helping your family with chores, you can find ways to make some extra coins! Ask your parents if you can do extra tasks or help them with their business. This will give you more coins to put into your magic money jar!

Re-align Your Assets

Picture your magic money jar growing into a treasure chest! Instead of keeping your coins in a little savings box with low returns, find a better place for them. Ask grown-ups to help you put your coins where they can grow faster, like in a piggy bank that gives you more coins over time!

Avoid the Credit Trap

Credit cards can be like borrowing magic, but they can also be tricky. Try using cash or your magic money jar when you buy things. That way, you'll only spend what you have, and you won't owe any coins later!

Setting Goals and Having a Plan

Setting goals and having a plan is like embarking on a treasure hunt to uncover your dreams. Imagine your dreams as precious gems waiting to be discovered. You can set goals to achieve them, whether it's buying something special or going on an exciting trip. But how do you reach those dreams? That's where your treasure map comes in. It's your game plan to success.

In your treasure map, you outline the steps you need to take to reach your goals. Just like a pirate following a map to find buried treasure, your map guides you on your journey to financial success. But remember, managing your finances is a bit like running a business, there are things you can control and things you can't.

In any business, there are factors beyond your control, like market changes or unexpected challenges. Similarly, in your financial journey, you might face unexpected expenses or economic shifts that you can't predict. But here's the good news. There are plenty of things you can control too.

Let's take a look at these key elements you can control:

- Budgeting: You have control over how you spend your money. Creating a budget helps you manage your income and expenses, making sure you're on track to achieve your goals.
- Saving: You decide how much you save. Putting money aside regularly helps you build a safety net for unexpected situations and work towards your dreams.
- Investing: You have the power to invest your money wisely. Learning about different investment options and making informed decisions can grow your wealth over time.
- Learning: Just like in a business, staying informed is essential. Educate yourself about personal finance, investments, and strategies to make smart choices.
- Debt Management: You can control how you manage debt. Being responsible with loans and credit cards keeps your financial health in check.
- Setting Goals: Your dreams are your goals. You have the ability to set clear and achievable goals that motivate you to take action.

- Adaptability: Life is full of surprises, and you can control how you adapt to changes. Having flexibility in your financial plan helps you navigate unexpected twists.

By focusing on these aspects, you take the reins of your financial journey. Just like a business owner steering their ship, you're in charge of your financial ship. And while you can't control everything, your proactive approach ensures you're prepared for the journey ahead.

Pay Yourself First

In life and business, many individuals struggle to save money at the end of the month due to various expenses and financial commitments. However, a simple and effective solution to this problem is to prioritize saving by adopting the "Pay Yourself First" approach. Here's how it works:

The Problem: The Month Is Longer Than the Money

Most people don't have enough to last until the end of the month. Imagine Trying this, at the first of the month, before you pay anyone else, write a check to yourself for 10% of your income.

The Solution: Pay Yourself First

This solution involves making savings a top priority in your financial planning. Instead of waiting until the end of the month to see if there's anything left to save, commit to saving a specific percentage of your income right from the beginning. In both life and business, this practice can yield remarkable results.

By paying yourself first, you build a safety net for unexpected expenses and emergencies. In personal life, it ensures that you have funds available for any unforeseen circumstances. In business, having a reserve helps manage cash flow during challenging times. Prioritizing saving at the start of the month ensures that you consistently set aside money for your future goals. Whether it's for personal aspirations like buying a home or for business growth and investment, this approach fosters discipline and commitment to your financial objectives.

Knowing that you have already allocated a portion of your income to savings brings peace of mind. This reduces financial stress and empowers you to make better decisions for both your personal and professional life. Over time, regular savings can lead to significant wealth accumulation. Whether you're saving for retirement, expanding your business, or achieving personal milestones, paying yourself first sets the foundation for long-term financial success.

Embracing the "Pay Yourself First" principle reinforces a positive financial mindset. It demonstrates that you value your own financial well-being and prioritize your future goals. By following this simple yet powerful solution, you take control of your financial future in both life and business. Committing to saving at the beginning of each month cultivates a habit of responsible money management, ultimately leading to a more secure and prosperous future. Remember, your financial success is in your hands, and paying yourself first sets you on the path to achieve your dreams and aspirations!

Start Investing Early

Investing early can have a significant impact on your financial future, and it's essential to understand the benefits of getting started as soon as possible. It pays to start investing early. Time is critical. When you're young, you may not have a lot of money to invest, but that's why time is so critical. By starting to save and invest early, even with small amounts, you can harness the potential of compounding and end up with thousands of dollars in the long run. On the other hand, if you delay starting to save, you'll need to contribute much more later on to achieve the same results.

Start Now to Reach Your FUN Goal

If you aspire to be financially independent, the best course of action is to start investing now. Delaying your investment journey means you'll need to save more later to catch up. Time is on your side when you start early, giving your money more time to grow and accumulate wealth.

The Cost of Waiting

Waiting to begin your investment journey can have high costs in the long run. The more time you wait, the more you miss out on the potential growth of your money. By procrastinating, you may find yourself in a situation where you have to invest much larger sums to reach your financial goals.

While investing early can be highly beneficial, it's crucial to remember that all investments come with risks. The examples above assume a hypothetical 9% constant rate of return, but actual investments may fluctuate in value. You must carefully assess your risk tolerance, do your research, and diversify your investments to mitigate risks and maximize potential returns. Investing is a journey, and it requires careful planning and discipline. Set clear financial goals, create a budget, and allocate a portion of your income to investments. Regularly review your investment strategy and adapt it to your changing circumstances.

The key takeaway is this, start investing early to harness the power of time and compound interest. While you may not have a lot of money now, consistent and early investments can lead to substantial wealth in the future. Seize the opportunity to secure your financial independence and build a brighter financial future for yourself!

Understanding Compound Interest and Debt

Compound interest can be a double-edged sword. While it can work in your favor when building savings, it can also work against you when you have debt. When you carry debt and pay only the minimum balance on your credit cards, the power of compound interest starts to work against you. Each month, interest charges are added to the remaining principal, and your new balance becomes the principal plus the interest. This new amount gets compounded again and again, making it challenging to pay off your debt.

For instance, let's say you made a one-time $3,000 purchase with no additional purchases and decided to make only the minimum payments. It would take you a whopping 10 years to pay off the debt, and during that time, you could end up paying thousands of dollars in interest charges alone!

So, it's crucial to be mindful of compound interest when managing your finances. Building savings and investments can benefit from compound interest, while tackling debt aggressively can save you from falling into the trap of mounting interest charges. When it comes to credit card debt, there are two main types: revolving and fixed debt. Understanding the difference between these types is crucial for managing your finances effectively.

Revolving Debt

Credit card debt is an example of revolving debt. With revolving debt, the interest on your outstanding balance compounds on a daily basis, not just monthly. This means that the interest charges can add up quickly, and you may end up paying much more in interest over time. Unlike fixed debt, where you have a fixed monthly payment to pay off the debt over a set period, revolving debt does not have a fixed amount you pay each month. Instead, you have the option to pay the minimum balance, but this can lead to your debt lasting for an extended period, sometimes indefinitely. Moreover, with revolving debt, your interest rate can change at any time, leaving you vulnerable to unexpected increases in interest charges. Unfortunately, there is little you can do to control or negotiate interest rate changes, except for paying off the entire balance at once. To avoid getting caught in a cycle of mounting debt, it's essential to be cautious with revolving debt and strive to pay off the balance in full each month whenever possible. Keeping a close eye on interest rates and making regular, timely payments can also help you manage your credit card debt more effectively.

Paying Off the Loan in Less Than 15 Years

To pay off the loan in full in less than 15 years, you can increase your monthly payment by about $200 (or more, depending on the exact loan terms). By doing this, you accelerate your principal reduction and reduce the overall interest paid. By paying more each month, you effectively shorten the loan term, saving over 60% in interest payments compared to a standard 30-year fixed mortgage. This allows you to become debt-free faster and save a substantial amount of money in interest costs. It's important to note that increasing your monthly payment requires careful consideration of your financial situation to ensure that you can comfortably afford the higher payments. Additionally, borrowers should check with their lenders to verify the specific loan terms and any prepayment penalties.

When it comes to managing your debts, finding the right payment strategy can significantly impact your financial journey. Your choice should consider your goals, budget, and priorities. By evaluating various payment options and their potential savings, you can make an informed decision that aligns with your long-term financial objectives. Before settling on a payment schedule, take a moment to assess your financial situation and your future aspirations. If you find that biweekly payments are comfortably manageable and you're aiming to minimize interest costs, this approach could be advantageous. On the other hand, if maintaining a predictable budget is more crucial to you, then opting for monthly payments might be the preferred route. Whichever path you choose, understanding the consequences of your payment frequency is crucial for effective long-term debt management.

Debt Stacking

Let's delve into a powerful strategy known as debt stacking, a systematic approach to tackling your debts and working your way towards financial freedom. Having a clear game plan for overcoming financial hurdles. Imagine each of your debts as a hurdle on a racetrack. Instead of trying to leap over all the hurdles simultaneously, which can be overwhelming, debt stacking encourages you to focus on clearing one hurdle at a time. This method breaks down the journey into manageable steps, making your path to financial independence less daunting and more achievable.

Here's How It Works

You list out your debts (what you owe), like credit cards or loans, and sort them by interest rates and amounts. Then, you target the first debt on your list, the one with the highest interest rate, for example. This is your "target account." You put extra effort into paying off this debt while making minimum payments on others. Once you pay off the target account, you shift the money you were using to pay it off and apply it to the next debt on your list. This keeps the momentum going. Progress keeps moving forward.

By focusing on the high-interest debts first, you're saving yourself from paying extra in interest over time. Plus, debt stacking ensures you always make the same total payment every month towards your debts, which makes budgeting simpler. It's essential not to take on new debts while you're working on clearing the old ones. It's like patching up a leaking boat while making sure no new leaks appear. As you pay off each debt, you'll feel a weightlifting off your shoulders. Once you're debt-free, the money you were using to pay off debts can now be redirected towards building your wealth. It's like switching gears from paying off past expenses to investing in your future. The benefits of understanding and using debt stacking are clear: you're on the path to becoming debt-free and gaining financial independence. The journey might take time, but with each debt you clear, you're a step closer to your goal. Just think about the peace of mind and the financial security that comes with being debt-free – it's a journey worth taking!

Calculate Your Financial Unrestricted Number (FUN)

Your Financial Unrestricted Number (FUN) Goal is a crucial step in achieving your desired lifestyle without financial stress. It represents the amount required to support your chosen lifestyle, providing you with the freedom and peace of mind you deserve. By calculating this number, you'll have a clear target to work towards and a solid foundation for your financial journey.

Here's How to Calculate Your FUN Goal

Assess Your Current Annual Expenses: This includes everything you spend on essentials like housing, utilities, groceries, transportation, healthcare, and other necessary costs. Be thorough in your evaluation to ensure accuracy.

Factor in Discretionary Spending: Consider any discretionary spending that contributes to your desired quality of life, such as entertainment, dining out, travel, and hobbies. These are the expenses that make life enjoyable and fulfilling.

Account for Inflation: Anticipate the impact of inflation over time. While your expenses may be at a certain level today, they are likely to increase over the years. A conservative estimate of inflation is typically around 2-3% annually.

Apply the 4% Rule: The 4% rule is a widely recognized guideline in financial planning. It suggests that if you can safely withdraw 4% of your investment portfolio each year, your funds should last throughout your lifetime. To calculate your FUN Goal, divide your total annual expenses by 0.04 (4%).

Formula: FUN Goal = Total Annual Expenses / 0.04

Example

Let's say your annual expenses amount to $60,000.

FUN Goal = $60,000 / 0.04 = $1,500,000

In this example, your FUN Goal is $1,500,000. This represents the total amount you need to have invested in income-producing assets to sustain your chosen lifestyle indefinitely. Keep in mind that this calculation provides a baseline estimate, and your actual financial situation may have unique factors to consider. Regularly review and adjust your FUN Goal as your circumstances change and as you move closer to achieving your financial goals.

By knowing your FUN Goal, you'll be equipped with a clear target, a roadmap to financial freedom, and the confidence to make informed decisions about your finances. Start your journey toward financial independence today! Determining your FUN Goal is a crucial step in achieving success and stability in both life and business. Just like knowing your weight can help you monitor your health, understanding your financial position empowers you to take control of your financial future.

Many of us shy away from assessing our current financial situation, much like avoiding stepping on a scale when we suspect we may have gained weight. However, without measuring where we stand, it's challenging to set clear targets and make progress. As the wise saying goes, "You can't hit a target you cannot see, and you cannot see a target you do not have" (Zig Ziglar). To embark on this journey towards financial freedom, you must identify a numerical target that represents your desired lifestyle. What amount of money will make you feel financially secure and fulfilled? Is it $500,000, $1 million, $10 million, or more? This figure will be unique to your aspirations and lifestyle.

If you currently live within your means, have a stable job or business, and rely on government or welfare support for your retirement, calculating your FUN Goal might seem like a mere intellectual exercise. However, if you find yourself in an uncertain job or business market, with doubts about government support, and a desire for full control over your financial future, determining your numeric financial goal becomes paramount. Having a specific target provides you with a clear direction to work towards.

Your FUN Goal is a result of factors such as your financial aspirations, your present and future lifestyle, and the performance of the investments you choose. By understanding these elements, you can set a realistic and achievable financial goal and chart a path towards securing it. Take the time to calculate your FUN Goal and start building a stable and prosperous financial future for both your life and business. Remember, having a clear target makes the journey more purposeful and the results more rewarding.

Understanding the Importance of Credit

Today, we'll be discussing the importance of valuing your credit and understanding how it can significantly impact your financial future. Credit is like a financial reputation that you build over time based on how responsibly you handle borrowed money. It's essential because it affects your ability to get loans, credit cards, and even influences landlords when you're looking to rent a place. Good credit can open doors to better opportunities, while bad credit can create obstacles and limit your financial options.

Let's delve into the significance of good credit and its impact on your financial life.

Good Credit

- Better Loan Terms: When you have good credit, banks and lenders see you as a low-risk borrower. As a result, you may qualify for loans with lower interest rates and better terms.

For example, if you need a car loan, having good credit could save you thousands of dollars in interest over the life of the loan.
- Lower Insurance Premiums: Believe it or not, some insurance companies use credit scores to determine your premiums. Good credit may result in lower insurance costs, such as auto and home insurance.
- Credit Card Perks: With good credit, you're more likely to be approved for credit cards with excellent rewards, cash-back offers, and travel benefits. These perks can save you money and add value to your financial management.
- Renting an Apartment: Many landlords check credit scores before approving rental applications. Having good credit can increase your chances of securing your desired apartment or rental property.

Bad Credit

- Difficulty Getting Approved for Loans: If you have a history of late payments or defaults, banks and lenders may see you as a higher risk and be less willing to approve you for loans or credit cards. If they do approve, it may come with higher interest rates.
- Higher Interest Rates: Even if you manage to get approved for a loan with bad credit, you'll likely face higher interest rates, increasing the overall cost of borrowing.
- Limit Financial Opportunities: Bad credit can limit your ability to start a business, buy a home, or pursue other significant financial goals.
- Difficulty Renting: As mentioned earlier, landlords often check credit scores. Bad credit may result in difficulty finding a suitable rental property.

Building and Maintaining Good Credit

To build and maintain good credit, it's essential to make payments on time, avoid maxing out credit cards, and only borrow what you can afford to repay. Your credit history is a reflection of your financial responsibility, and taking care of it can lead to more opportunities and financial security in the future. Remember, building good credit is a process that takes time and consistent financial habits, but it's an investment in your financial well-being. Start early, be responsible, and you'll be on the path to a strong credit profile that will serve you well in your future endeavors.

Mutual Funds: A Smart Investment Choice

Mutual funds can be an excellent choice for individuals and families looking to invest in the economy while minimizing risk. Let's dive deeper into why mutual funds are considered a great option for many investors.

Advantages of Mutual Funds

- Ownership and Diversification: When you invest in a mutual fund, you become a partial owner of a diverse portfolio of assets, such as stocks, bonds, or a combination of both. This diversification spreads the risk across various investments, reducing the impact of poor performance from any single asset.
- Professional Management: One of the key advantages of mutual funds is that they are managed by professional fund managers. These experts analyze market trends, study companies, and make investment decisions on behalf of the fund, aiming to achieve the best possible returns for investors.
- Accessibility for Average Families: Mutual funds provide an opportunity for average families to participate in the stock

market and other investment opportunities that may have been difficult to access individually. By pooling money together, mutual funds create a collective investment vehicle that opens the door to a broader range of assets.
- Risk Management: While there is inherent risk in any investment, mutual funds offer a level of risk management through diversification and professional management. This can help mitigate the impact of market volatility and fluctuations.
- Potential for Attractive Returns: Although past performance doesn't guarantee future results, mutual funds historically have offered competitive rates of return compared to traditional savings accounts or other conservative investment options.
- Flexibility and Choices: Mutual funds come in various types, allowing investors to choose funds that align with their financial goals, risk tolerance, and time horizon. Whether it's growth funds, income funds, or balanced funds, there's a mutual fund that suits different investment needs.

However, it's important to remember that no investment is entirely risk-free, and mutual funds are no exception. As the economy fluctuates and market conditions change, the value of mutual fund shares can go up or down. It's essential for investors to do their research, understand the investment strategy of the mutual fund, and assess their own risk tolerance before investing.

Overall, mutual funds provide a valuable opportunity for individuals and families to participate in the growth of the economy while having their investments professionally managed. They offer a balance between risk and reward, making them a popular choice for those seeking to build wealth and achieve financial goals over the long term.

The Strategy for Achieving Financial Freedom

The strategy for achieving financial freedom is not a mystery or hidden secret; it requires a combination of mindset and technical skills. Financial success is primarily influenced by 80% soft skills, such as mindset and financial attitudes, and 20% technical skills related to money management, investing, and entrepreneurship. To attain a strong financial outlook, you must effectively allocate and manage your present and future financial resources, aligning them with your values and desired lifestyle.

CHAPTER TEN

Financial Success & Your Future

Imagine your financial journey as a grand expedition, with debt as the treacherous terrain you must conquer. It's time to face these challenges head-on and reclaim control. Start by understanding your debt landscape: who you owe, how much, and the interest rates. With this map in hand, chart a clear path to repayment. Whether you choose the avalanche method (tackling high-interest debt first) or the snowball method (starting with smaller debts), a well-defined strategy will steer you through the rough terrain.

Picture your credit score as the North Star, guiding your financial voyage. Keep a vigilant watch over it. A strong credit score opens doors to favorable terms and opportunities. Stay on course by paying bills promptly, maintaining low credit card balances, and avoiding unnecessary new accounts. Just like the steady guidance of the North Star, a healthy credit score ensures you're on the right track.

Think of financial stability as your ultimate destination and your financial plan as the compass that guides you there. Develop a budget that balances spending, saving, and investing. Establish an emergency fund to weather unexpected storms, and consider investments for your future, whether in retirement accounts, stocks, or real estate. While the journey may present twists and turns, a well-prepared plan ensures you're equipped for any challenges that arise.

Imagine the alluring shores of impulsive spending and instant gratification. While they may beckon, these paths often lead to rocky terrain. Stay focused on your financial objectives and steer clear of splurges that could derail your progress. Practice delayed gratification, make informed investments, and remember that true financial security is the ultimate reward.

Let this chapter serve as your navigation guide through the vast financial sea. From managing debt to maintaining good credit and securing your financial future, it's about setting your sights on the horizon and plotting a course that aligns with your goals. Think of yourself as the captain of your financial ship. You're the decision-maker at the helm, determining the course of your journey. As you sail through this chapter, keep in mind that each choice you make shapes your financial trajectory. It's time to embrace the wisdom of sound financial decisions and set sail toward a future marked by stability, security, and prosperity.

Build a Supportive Network

Welcome to the world of optimism, where aspirations materialize through actions, not just hopes. In this chapter, we shed light on an age-old truth. The people you associate with influence your path. Prepare to embrace the influence of positivity and how it can drive you closer to your ambitions.

Imagine your journey as a road trip taken with companions who influence your adventure. Positive people are more than just dreamers; they're active individuals who inject enthusiasm into your ambitions. They support your goals, have faith in your skills, and strengthen your determination. Think of positive thinking as your guiding force. It merges optimism with action, creating a driving energy that pushes you forward. Positivity goes beyond words; it's a dedication to acting, partnering with you to achieve shared dreams.

Picture this, you're destined to soar like an eagle, yet you're encircled by chickens content on the ground. Now comes the choice, remain within the coop or soar freely in the air? Positive people are like flying aside fellow eagles, poised to ascend to greater heights. Their enthusiasm, determination, and confidence in what's achievable bolster your flight toward accomplishment.

Think of gathering a community of kindred spirits who champion your vision. These are individuals who share your dreams or are on parallel journeys of growth. They act as your supporters, sounding boards, and collaborators on the path of progress. Surrounding yourself with this tribe establishes a robust support system that bolsters your determination.

So, fellow dreamers, bear in mind that this chapter serves as your handbook for harnessing the uplifting influence of your community. As you initiate your voyage, acknowledge that your company holds significance. Positive individuals become the wind beneath your wings, lifting your dreams to newfound altitudes.

The Power of Saving

Welcome to the realm of smart savers! In this chapter, we delve into the timeless wisdom of Benjamin Franklin and his golden rule: "A penny saved is a penny earned." Get ready to uncover the enchantment of saving and how those humble pennies can metamorphose into a treasure chest of financial opportunities.

Imagine your money as a puzzle, each penny a crucial piece. Franklin's words remind us that saving these pennies isn't just about stashing them away; it's about their inherent value. Just like earning, saving is a method to enhance your financial worth. It's a small yet potent stride on your path to financial empowerment.

Envision your savings as your secret asset. It's a safety net, shielding you from unexpected costs or rainy days. Every penny you save constructs a foundation for financial stability. So, amid your earnings, remember to accumulate those pennies, for they are the bedrock of your financial future.

Picture this: as you begin saving, every penny finds its place in your savings account. Over time, these pennies aren't idle spectators; they grow. Compound interest acts like a magical charm, converting your modest savings into a bountiful harvest. The more you save, the more these pennies labor for you, initiating a snowball effect of financial expansion.

Imagine saving as a habit, just like brushing your teeth. Start small but maintain consistency. Allocate a portion of your income, be it 5%, 10%, or whatever suits your savings. The key lies in making saving an unbreakable part of your financial routine. Before you know it, those pennies will aggregate into dollars, and those dollars will multiply into actualized dreams.

So, fellow savers, remember that this chapter serves as your compass to embrace the influence of saving. Benjamin Franklin's wisdom reminds us that modest strides can lead to immense leaps in your financial voyage. Every penny saved is an investment in your future, a future enriched with opportunities seized, dreams fulfilled, and financial freedom.

Imagine yourself as a curator of pennies, each one emblematic of a step nearer to your financial aspirations. It's time to amass those pennies, witness their growth, and savor the gratification of molding a stable base for your financial prosperity. As you embrace the enchantment of saving, recall that every penny carries significance, and each stride you take today constructs a platform for a brighter and more financially stable tomorrow.

Plugging the Leaks

Let's embark on a journey inspired by Benjamin Franklin's timeless wisdom: "Beware of little expenses. A small leak will sink a great ship." Prepare to take the helm of your financial vessel, plugging those small leaks and steering away from turbulent financial currents.

Envision your finances as a sturdy ship sailing the seas of life. Franklin's words remind us that even minor leaks can lead to disaster. Seemingly inconsequential expenses may accumulate and burden your financial ship. It's time to assume control and prevent these leaks from evolving into a sinking situation.

Consider small expenses as the "latte factor." Daily coffee or occasional snacks may appear trivial, yet they can accrue over time. These choices, innocuous as they seem, can deplete your finances more rapidly than you anticipate. By recognizing and curbing these leaks, you're freeing resources to invest in your aspirations and fortify your financial prospects.

Picture yourself as a resourceful sailor equipped with financial tools. It's time to mend leaks, patch gaps, and forestall future issues. Begin by meticulously tracking your expense, every detail counts. Once you pinpoint the culprits, assess which ones can be trimmed or eliminated. This may entail small sacrifices today for smoother financial sailing ahead.

Imagine your financial ship with two crew members: one spends, the other saves. The spender lets money slip through like sand, while the saver amasses treasure in the ship's vault. Over time, compounding effects transform this treasure into a substantial wealth reserve. By managing expenses, you're ensuring your financial vessel remains buoyant and thriving.

So, fellow financial mariners, recognize that this chapter equips you with tools to seal leaks and navigate your financial journey with finesse. Benjamin Franklin's insight underscores that minor leaks can lead to significant consequences. By mastering the art of expense management, you're not just averting financial peril; you're seizing control of your destiny.

Visualize yourself as the captain charting a course to safer shores. Be vigilant, identify leaks, and proactively prevent them from disrupting your financial voyage. As you sail towards financial stability, remember that each choice you make today propels you toward calmer waters and brighter prospects.

Exploring Financial Security

Let's venture into the realm of financial security, guided by Warren Buffett's wisdom: "Rule No. 1, Never lose money. Rule No. 2, Never forget rule No. 1." Prepare to become the guardians of your financial realm as we delve into essential strategies to shield your wealth from harm.

Envision Warren Buffett as a sage presenting you with a sacred scroll etched upon it are two unwavering principles. His insight underscores that safeguarding wealth isn't merely an option; it's a mandate. These rules aren't casual advice; they're the bedrock of a resilient fortress that stands strong against the uncertainties of finance.

Imagine yourself as the vigilant protector, entrusted with preserving your financial heritage. It's time to arm yourself with an array of strategies. These tools will assist you in repelling potential risks, navigating economic downturns, and managing unforeseen challenges. By mastering these tools, you're not just safeguarding your money; you're securing your peace of mind.

Visualize constructing a moat around your fortress of wealth. The strategies to shield your money are like the stones of that moat, forming a barrier against threats. Diversification, insurance, emergency funds, risk management, and prudent investments are these stones. Each one fortifies your financial stronghold.

Consider these strategies as your financial safety net. Life's unpredictability can bring unexpected storms. By establishing a robust defense mechanism, you ensure your wealth remains intact even in adversity. These strategies offer resilience, enabling you to navigate challenges while upholding your financial stability.

So, fellow stewards of wealth, know that this chapter is your guide to fortifying your financial haven. Warren Buffett's words emphasize that protection isn't merely a tactic, it's a way of life for your money. Abiding by the principles of never losing money doesn't just build wealth, it safeguards it.

Imagine yourself as the commander of your financial fortress, overseeing the construction of a robust defense system. It's time to put into practice strategies aligned with Buffett's teachings. By doing so, you craft a legacy of security for yourself and future generations. As you embrace the art of safeguarding your money, remember that every decision you make today lays a brick in the fortress of your financial future.

Embracing the Journey of Homeownership

In this chapter, a journey unfolds, one that resonates with the heart and soul of the American dream: homeownership. Guided by Wendell Pierce's words, "That is the heart and soul of the American dream, homeownership, the idea of being able to buy a house and start to build your family," we delve into the significance of having a place to call your own.

Envision your home as the canvas of your life's story. Wendell Pierce's insight reminds us that homeownership goes beyond shelter; it's about sowing the seeds of a future, building a legacy, and crafting a haven where memories find their place.

See yourself as an explorer mapping the path to your own slice of the American dream. It's time to uncover the routes that lead to homeownership. From saving for a down payment to navigating mortgage choices, each step advances you towards unlocking the door to your very own abode.

View your home as more than just a residence; it's an investment in your present and future. Homeownership bestows stability, a sense of belonging, and the freedom to infuse your space with your style. It's where you create memories, express yourself, and establish a sanctuary for yourself and your loved ones.

Imagine passing down the keys to your home to the next generation, a legacy to cherish. Your home becomes woven into your family's history, a place where stories unite, and connections strengthen. Beyond walls, it stands as a testament to your dedication, dreams, and the love you've poured into every corner.

Wendell Pierce's words underscore the transformation of the American dream of homeownership into reality. A home encompasses aspirations and becomes the heart of your journey. By embracing the path to homeownership, you're not just acquiring a dwelling; you're laying the foundation for your family's future.

Picture yourself as the architect of your aspirations, sketching blueprints for a place that holds your dreams. It's time to navigate the trails, overcome hurdles, and turn homeownership into reality. As you step forward, remember that each stride today brings you closer to the threshold of "home sweet home."

Preparing for Your Golden Years

Let's delve into the art of preparing for your golden years, guided by the wisdom of George S. Clason: "Prepare for your old age by starting to save and invest money for the future. Work hard to improve your skills and ensure a future income because wealth is the result of a reliable income stream." Brace yourself to nurture the seeds of financial security that will flourish into a comfortable retirement.

Imagine your financial future as a thriving garden, where each plant signifies the fruits of your labor. George S. Clason's wisdom underscores that readying for old age isn't just a task; it's a mission to make the years ahead abundant and rewarding.

See yourself as the attentive gardener, planting the seeds of financial abundance. It's time to begin saving and investing for the future. Whether through retirement accounts, emergency funds, or investment ventures, each move today tends to your financial garden's growth.

Think of yourself as the adept horticulturist tending to the growth of your wealth. Continuously improving your skills and knowledge is crucial. This not only ensures a dependable income but also cultivates opportunities that will bloom throughout your life.

Imagine reaching old age with the contentment of knowing you've reaped what you've sown. Your consistent efforts in saving, investing, and skill enhancement have yielded a reliable income stream, a cornerstone of your wealth. This foundation grants security and freedom to relish your well-deserved retirement.

Fellow cultivators of wealth, know that this chapter is your guide for sowing the seeds of financial security in your golden years. George S. Clason's wisdom underscores that wealth isn't fleeting; it's the outcome of intentional action and thoughtful planning. By embracing the art of preparing for old age, you're not just securing your future; you're embracing the delight of harvesting the rewards of your labor.

View yourself as the steward of your financial garden, nurturing it with care and dedication. It's time to save, invest, and refine your skills, understanding that each decision you make today contributes to the garden that will sustain you in your golden years. As you embark on this journey, remember that the future you nurture today will blossom into the abundance you'll enjoy tomorrow.

The Simple Math of Retirement Income

Retirement planning can feel overwhelming, but there's a simple rule of thumb that can help you estimate how much money you need to retire comfortably. Imagine having a specific monthly income in mind for your retirement years. Let's say it's $5,000. Now, the rule is easy: multiply that monthly income goal by 300 or 200, depending on how you want to approach risk and returns.

For instance, with the rule of 300, if you desire a $5,000 monthly retirement income, multiply it by 300. The result, $1,500,000, is the amount you'd ideally have saved up. This approach assumes an average 4% return on your investments. In this scenario, your investments generate about $5,000 each month, leaving your initial $1,500,000 untouched.

Alternatively, using the rule of 200, you would multiply $5,000 by 200, which equals $1,000,000. With a slightly higher risk tolerance and an assumed 6% return, your $1 million invested would provide the same $5,000 monthly income without depleting the original amount.

These rules offer a simplified starting point for retirement planning, but remember, life isn't always so straightforward. They don't account for factors like inflation, taxes, or unexpected expenses that can impact your retirement income.

Here's the life lesson, by understanding these basic rules, you gain a practical perspective on how to approach retirement savings. Let's explore the benefits of grasping these concepts and how they can elevate your financial planning to the next level.

Understanding these simple rules helps you set a tangible goal for your retirement fund. It gives you a benchmark to work towards and a sense of how your current savings align with your desired retirement lifestyle. This knowledge empowers you to take actionable steps to either save more or adjust your expectations, ensuring you're on the right track for a comfortable retirement.

Moreover, grasping these rules helps you communicate more effectively with financial advisors. When you have a baseline understanding of how much you need and how investment returns play a role, you can engage in more meaningful discussions about your retirement strategy. This collaborative approach allows you to tailor your plan to your unique circumstances, risk tolerance, and goals.

So, whether you're just starting your career or are closer to retirement age, understanding these simple rules can guide your financial decisions. They provide clarity, a starting point, and a foundation for informed retirement planning. As you build your financial future, keep in mind that knowledge is power, and by understanding these principles, you're better equipped to make choices that lead to a comfortable and fulfilling retirement.

Taking the Leap: Embrace Risk and Shape Your Financial Destiny

Are you ready to elevate your financial IQ? This chapter is all about stepping out of your comfort zone and seizing control of your financial future. Picture this, you're at a crossroads. On one side is the familiar path of the 9-to-5 grind, playing it safe, and hoping things will magically fall into place. On the other side is the thrilling unknown, taking risks, expanding your horizons, and mastering the art of financial intelligence.

You have two choices: dive headfirst into the world of financial education, embracing risk like a pro, or stick to the status quo, hoping your boss, the government, and the bank will be your financial saviors. But here's the thing, the landscape is changing, and relying solely on others might not cut it anymore.

It's like being on a ship in the vast sea of life. You can choose to be a passenger, letting someone else steer the ship, or you can be the captain, navigating your vessel to uncharted territories. That's where financial IQ comes into play. It's your compass, your map, and your secret weapon.

Sure, the comfort zone is cozy, but guess what? The most beautiful views come after a daring climb. Taking calculated risks is like stepping onto a new continent of possibilities. Investing in assets, starting a business, or exploring new income streams might be unfamiliar territory, but it's where the magic happens.

Let's talk about the price you might have to pay. Yes, it's effort, time, and sometimes stepping into the unknown. But isn't it worth it for the promise of financial freedom and empowerment? Imagine shaping a future where you're not just surviving but thriving, where you're not just living within your means but expanding your means.

So, my fellow risk-takers, the choice is yours. Will you embrace the challenge, pay the price, and secure your financial future? Or will you stay in your comfort bubble, hoping for the best? Remember, the signs of the times are pointing toward taking control of your destiny. It's time to write your financial story, one bold decision at a time. The question isn't whether you're willing, it's whether you're ready for the adventure of a lifetime.

A New Beginning

As this shared journey comes to an end, it's time to reflect on the wisdom, inspiration, and empowerment gained. This chapter marks not just a conclusion, but a fresh start, a launchpad for your financial dreams. Let's step into this final phase with hope, determination, and the understanding that your future lies within your hands.

Think of this moment as turning a page, not just in a book, but in your life. You've walked alongside insights, perspectives, and guidance. Your dedication to financial growth and empowerment illuminates a path leading to brighter days.

Throughout this journey, you've immersed yourself in financial understanding, grasping the significance of saving, investing, mindful spending, and embracing emotional intelligence while tending to your financial well-being. It's about progress, not perfection. Each step taken, every insight absorbed, builds a foundation for success.

Consider this journey a roadmap, a resource to revisit for guidance, inspiration, or a gentle push. The lessons learned here equip you for the journey's twists and turns. Like a compass pointing the way, your newfound knowledge guides you toward your goals.

As you close this chapter and step into the world, remember you hold the pen to your financial story. Your dreams, aspirations, and actions shape your narrative. Challenges and victories await, accompanied by growth. Yet through it all, you hold the power to craft your own tale.

The world awaits your embrace of potential, seizing opportunities, and ongoing pursuit of financial empowerment. Remember, the power to effect change and create your desired life resides within you. Your financial horizon gleams, illuminated by the lessons you've learned. From these pages, thank you for allowing these words to accompany you on your quest for financial progress. Know you're not alone on this journey, countless others walk alongside, driven by similar desires.

With a heart full of hope and a mind armed with wisdom, step boldly into the next chapter of life. Embrace challenges, celebrate victories, and maintain a spirit of learning, growth, and evolution. Your financial journey attests to your determination, resilience, and commitment to your success.

Here's to you. To a future rich with prosperity, contentment, and the delight of realizing dreams. Your journey is just commencing, and the best is yet to come. Wishing you all the success and happiness the world holds. Remember, surround yourself with positive-minded individuals!

Positive thinking isn't mere wishful thoughts. It's anchored in action, and the energy of those who believe in and support your dreams is palpable. Associate with those who elevate you, for eagles soar in the company of eagles, not chickens. Seek out like-minded individuals who share your vision or strive to grow alongside you.

Lastly, believe in yourself! Stepping out of your comfort zone can seem daunting, and some may not support your dreams, even close ones. When faced with doubt, ask if your financial freedom is worth the present price. If the answer is no, act now. Write down your aspirations, share them with a positive confidant, and take that initial step. Regret won't be a part of the equation.

Cultivating Intangible Assets

Generational wealth extends beyond financial assets; it encompasses the transmission of intangible qualities that shape the character and success of future generations. We will explore the importance of cultivating intangible assets within your family and how to pass them on effectively.

At the heart of generational wealth are the values that define your family's identity and guide its actions. Instilling core values such as integrity, responsibility, and compassion lays the groundwork for future success. Encourage open discussions about values within your family, and lead by example to demonstrate their importance in everyday life.

A strong work ethic is essential for achieving success in any endeavor. Teach your children the value of hard work, perseverance, and determination from a young age. Provide opportunities for them to take on responsibilities and experience the satisfaction of accomplishing tasks through effort and diligence.

Education is a powerful tool for personal and professional growth. Prioritize education within your family, encouraging lifelong learning and intellectual curiosity. Support your children's academic pursuits and provide resources for their continued education, whether through formal schooling, mentorship, or self-directed learning.

Emotional intelligence, including self-awareness, empathy, and resilience, is crucial for navigating life's challenges and building meaningful relationships.

"It's not what you leave to your children, it's what you leave in them."

-Bishop T.D. Jakes

Teach your children to recognize and manage their emotions effectively and encourage them to develop empathy and compassion for others. Provide opportunities for them to practice resilience and adaptability in the face of adversity.

Mentorship and guidance from experienced individuals can significantly impact a person's personal and professional development. Foster mentorship relationships within your family and encourage your children to seek guidance from trusted mentors and role models. Create opportunities for intergenerational learning and sharing of wisdom and experience.

Encourage a culture of personal development within your family, where individuals are committed to continuous growth and improvement. Support your children in setting and pursuing personal goals and provide resources and encouragement for their self-development journey. Emphasize the importance of self-reflection, goal-setting, and ongoing self-improvement.

By actively cultivating these intangible assets within your family, you lay a strong foundation for generational wealth and success. As you instill core values, foster a strong work ethic, prioritize education, cultivate emotional intelligence, facilitate mentorship, and promote personal development, you empower future generations to thrive and contribute positively to the world around them.

Navigating Family Dynamics

Passing on generational wealth involves more than just managing financial assets; it also requires navigating the complex dynamics of family relationships. We will explore strategies for fostering open communication, resolving conflicts, and promoting unity within your family as you work to build and preserve your legacy.

Effective communication is essential for maintaining strong family relationships and ensuring everyone feels heard and valued. Encourage open dialogue within your family, creating a safe space for members to express their thoughts, feelings, and concerns. Foster a culture of active listening, empathy, and mutual respect, where each family member's perspective is valued and considered.

Conflicts are inevitable in any family, but how they are resolved can either strengthen or strain relationships. Teach your family members conflict resolution skills, emphasizing the importance of addressing issues openly, respectfully, and constructively. Encourage compromise, negotiation, and seeking common ground to find mutually satisfactory solutions.

Unity and collaboration are essential for achieving shared goals and objectives as a family. Foster a sense of unity and common purpose among family members, emphasizing the importance of working together towards common goals. Encourage collaboration and teamwork, leveraging the unique strengths and talents of each family member to achieve collective success.

A family governance structure provides a framework for managing family affairs, making decisions, and preserving family values and traditions. Establish clear roles, responsibilities, and decision-making processes within your family governance structure, promoting transparency, accountability, and fairness. Consider creating a family council or board to oversee family matters and facilitate communication and decision-making.

Financial literacy is essential for effectively managing generational wealth and ensuring its preservation for future generations. Educate your family members about financial concepts, strategies, and best practices, empowering them to make informed decisions about money and investments. Instill a sense of financial responsibility and stewardship, emphasizing the importance of prudent financial management and long-term planning.

By actively addressing family dynamics and promoting unity, collaboration, and financial literacy, you lay a strong foundation for preserving and passing on your family's legacy.

Estate Planning and Legacy Preservation

Estate planning is a vital component of building and preserving generational wealth. We will delve into the significance of estate planning and discuss strategies for effectively preserving your legacy for future generations.

Estate planning involves making important decisions about the distribution of your assets and the management of your affairs in the event of your incapacity or death. It is essential for ensuring that your wishes are carried out, your loved ones are provided for, and your assets are protected. By creating a comprehensive estate plan, you can minimize taxes, avoid probate, and provide clarity and direction for your heirs.

A comprehensive estate plan typically includes various legal documents, such as a will, trust, power of attorney, and healthcare directives. Work with an experienced estate planning attorney to create a plan that addresses your unique circumstances and objectives. Consider factors such as the size and complexity of your estate, the needs of your beneficiaries, and your long-term goals for preserving your wealth.

One of the primary goals of estate planning is to protect your assets and minimize taxes. Explore strategies for reducing estate taxes, such as gifting assets during your lifetime, establishing trusts, and utilizing tax-advantaged investment vehicles. Consider the potential impact of estate taxes on your heirs and take steps to mitigate their tax burden.

Preserving your legacy involves more than just passing on financial assets; it also entails imparting your values, wisdom, and aspirations to future generations. Consider creating a family mission statement or legacy plan that outlines your family's core values, goals, and traditions. Educate your heirs about the importance of stewardship, philanthropy, and responsible wealth management.

As you plan for the transfer of your wealth to future generations, consider the broader impact of your financial decisions. Emphasize the importance of financial education, entrepreneurship, and charitable giving within your family. Encourage your heirs to be good stewards of their inheritance and to use their wealth to make a positive difference in the world.

By creating a comprehensive estate plan and emphasizing the importance of legacy preservation, you can ensure that your generational wealth endures for future generations.

Giving Back and Social Responsibility

True wealth extends beyond financial prosperity; it encompasses the impact we make on the world around us. Next, we will explore the significance of philanthropy, social responsibility, and community engagement in building a meaningful legacy. Discover how giving back can enrich your life and leave a lasting positive imprint on society.

Philanthropy is the act of giving back to others through charitable donations, volunteer work, or community service. It plays a crucial role in addressing social issues, supporting worthy causes, and improving the lives of those in need. By engaging in philanthropy, individuals and families can make a tangible difference in their communities and beyond.

Social responsibility entails taking accountability for the impact of your actions on society and the environment. It involves making ethical decisions, promoting sustainability, and supporting causes that align with your values. Embrace social responsibility as a guiding principle in your personal and professional life and strive to contribute positively to the well-being of others and the planet.

Charitable giving is an integral part of building a meaningful legacy. Identify causes and organizations that resonate with your family's values and interests and allocate resources to support them. Establish a charitable foundation, donor-advised fund, or charitable trust to formalize your giving efforts and maximize their impact over time. Involve your family in the philanthropic process, instilling values of generosity, empathy, and compassion in future generations.

Community engagement involves actively participating in initiatives and activities that benefit your local community. Volunteer your time and expertise to support local nonprofits, schools, or community organizations. Get involved in community clean-up efforts, neighborhood revitalization projects, or youth mentorship programs. By actively engaging in your community, you can forge meaningful connections, build social capital, and create positive change close to home.

As you embark on your philanthropic journey, strive to make a lasting impact that extends beyond financial contributions. Seek opportunities to address root causes of social issues, promote systemic change, and empower marginalized communities. Collaborate with other philanthropists, nonprofits, and community leaders to leverage resources and expertise for maximum impact. By working together, we can create a more just, equitable, and compassionate society for future generations.

Embracing Generational Prosperity

Congratulations on reaching the culmination of your journey to building generational wealth and prosperity! By following the strategies outlined in this book, you have taken significant steps towards creating a legacy that will endure for generations to come. As you reflect on your accomplishments, remember that generational prosperity encompasses more than just financial wealth; it encompasses the intangible qualities and opportunities you pass down to your descendants.

Take a moment to reflect on the journey you have undertaken to build generational prosperity. Consider the challenges you have overcome, the lessons you have learned, and the progress you have made towards your goals. Celebrate your achievements and acknowledge the growth you have experienced along the way.

Generational prosperity is built not only on financial assets but also on intangible assets such as values, wisdom, and opportunities. Reflect on the values you have instilled in your family, the wisdom you have shared, and the opportunities you have created for future generations. These intangible assets are invaluable components of your family's legacy.

As a steward of generational prosperity, embrace your responsibility to safeguard and nurture the wealth and values you have cultivated. Commit to upholding the principles of integrity, stewardship, and sustainability in managing your family's assets and legacy. By acting as a responsible steward, you ensure that your family's prosperity will endure for generations to come.

Prepare to pass the torch of generational prosperity to the next generation. Share your knowledge, wisdom, and experiences with your descendants, empowering them to carry forward the legacy you have built. Encourage open communication, collaboration, and shared decision-making among family members to ensure the continued growth and prosperity of your family's legacy.

Embrace the journey of building generational prosperity as an ongoing process of growth, learning, and evolution. Remain adaptable and open-minded as you navigate the complexities of managing wealth and legacy. Embrace change as an opportunity for innovation and renewal, and stay committed to the values and principles that guide your family's legacy.

Congratulations once again on reaching this significant milestone in your journey towards generational prosperity. By embracing the values of stewardship, integrity, and sustainability, you are laying the foundation for a legacy that will enrich the lives of your family members for generations to come. As you continue on your journey, remember to embrace the challenges and opportunities that lie ahead, and to cherish the legacy you are creating for future generations.

As we reach the end of our journey together through the pages of "Thriving, 'In the Black,'" it is time to reflect on the wealth of knowledge, insights, and strategies we have explored to empower you on your path to financial prosperity. Throughout this book, we have delved into the essential principles of financial management, the importance of cultivating generational wealth, and the transformative power of mindful stewardship.

As you close this chapter and embark on the next phase of your financial journey, I invite you to embrace the following key takeaways:

- Financial Empowerment: You hold the key to your financial success. By taking control of your finances, setting clear goals, and adopting disciplined financial habits, you can pave the way for a brighter financial future.
- Generational Wealth: Beyond monetary riches, generational wealth encompasses the values, wisdom, and opportunities you pass down to future generations. By nurturing these intangible assets, you create a legacy that transcends material wealth and enriches the lives of your descendants.
- Stewardship and Responsibility: As stewards of wealth and prosperity, it is our responsibility to manage our resources wisely, uphold ethical principles, and make decisions that benefit not only ourselves but also our communities and the world at large.
- Lifelong Learning: The journey to financial prosperity is a lifelong process of growth, learning, and adaptation. Stay curious, remain open to new ideas, and continually seek opportunities to enhance your financial knowledge and skills.
- Gratitude and Generosity: Cultivate an attitude of gratitude for the abundance in your life and practice generosity towards others. By giving back to your community and supporting causes you believe in, you contribute to the greater good and create a ripple effect of positive change.

As you bid farewell to these pages, remember that the journey to financial prosperity is not without its challenges. There will be setbacks, obstacles, and moments of uncertainty along the way. But by staying true to your values, remaining resilient in the face of adversity, and staying committed to your goals, you can overcome any challenge and emerge stronger and more prosperous than ever before.

I am honored to have been a part of your journey through "Thriving, 'In the Black.'" May the insights and wisdom shared within these pages serve as a guiding light on your path to financial prosperity. Remember, the power to thrive lies within you. Embrace it, nurture it, and let it guide you towards a future filled with abundance, prosperity, and fulfillment.

Wishing you all the best on your journey ahead.

-Dr. Robert S. Dayse

ABOUT THE AUTHOR

Dr. Robert S. Dayse's journey as an entrepreneur began early, launching his first venture selling sandwiches in elementary school. His business acumen was further refined with an MBA, setting the foundation for a career marked by innovation and leadership.

Dr. Dayse attended Howard University College of Dentistry, where he earned multiple awards, including the prestigious Award for Excellence in Oral Maxillofacial Surgery. His dedication to the field led him to serve as Chief Resident, professor, and attending physician at Howard University Hospital.

Deeply committed to his community, Dr. Dayse is passionate about providing affordable dental care through his management company, serving a broad spectrum of patients, including the underserved.

His commitment extends beyond local contributions, as he actively participates in international surgical missions with organizations like Surgeons for Smiles, broadening his impact on global dental health.

Dr. Dayse's expertise also spans the business sector. He has served as an advisor and investor in multiple startups, ranging from tech to brick-and-mortar establishments.

His innovative work in billing and coding practices at a Level I Trauma Center earned national recognition from the American Association of Oral and Maxillofacial Surgery.

An investor, commercial real estate owner, tech startup founder, business owner, and educator, Dr. Dayse continues to garner accolades as a respected professional.

He is also a devoted family man and community leader, dedicated to making a significant difference both locally and abroad.

Dr. Robert S. Dayse currently resides in historic Maryland, USA.

www.ingramcontent.com/pod-product-compliance
Lightning Source LLC
LaVergne TN
LVHW010156070526
838199LV00062B/4386